IN OUR C

BY

AGNES REPPLIER

Introduction

It has been many years since I went to school. Everything has changed in the Convent that I loved, and I am asked to believe that every change is for the better. I do not believe this at all. I am unmoved by the sight of steam registers and electric lights. I look with disfavour upon luxuries which would have seemed to us like the opulence of Aladdin's palace. I cannot wax enthusiastic over the intrusion of Mr. Matthew Arnold and Mr. Pater upon the library shelves, where Chambers' Miscellany used to be *our* nearest approach to the intellectual. The old order changes, and that unlovely word, modernity, is heard within the tranquil convent walls. Even the iron hand of discipline has been relaxed; for the long line of girls whom I now watch filing sedately in and out of the chapel have been taught to rule themselves, to use their wider liberty with discretion. I wonder how they like it. I wonder if liberty, coupled with discretion, is worth having when one is eleven years old. I wonder if it be the part of wisdom to be wise so soon.

The friends whom I loved are scattered far and wide. When Tony died, she took with her the sound of laughter into the silent land, and all things have seemed more sober since she left. To those who live, these pages will, I hope, bring back the sentiment of our early days. We made one another's world then,—a world full of adventures, and imaginings, and sweet absurdities that no one of us would now wish less absurd. Our successors to-day know more than we knew (they could not well know less), they have lectures, and enamelled bathtubs, and "Essays in Criticism;" but do they live their lives as vehemently as we lived ours; do they hold the secrets of childhood inviolate in their hearts as we held them in ours; are they as untainted by the commonplace, as remote from the obvious, as we always were; and will they have as vivid a picture of their convent days to look back upon, as the one we look at now?

A. R.

Marianus

I do not know how Marianus ever came to leave his native land, nor what turn of fate brought him to flutter the dovecotes of a convent school. At eleven, one does not often ask why things happen, because nothing seems strange enough to provoke the question. It was enough for me—it was enough for all of us—that one Sunday morning he appeared in little Peter's place, lit the candles on the altar, and served Mass with decent and devout propriety. Our customary torpor of cold and sleepiness—Mass was at seven, and the chapel unheated—yielded to a warm glow of excitement. I craned my white-veiled head (we wore black veils throughout the week and white on Sundays) to see how Elizabeth was taking this delightful novelty. *She* was busy passing her prayer-book, with something evidently written on the fly-leaf, to Emily Goring on the bench ahead. Emily, oblivious of consequences, was making telegraphic signals to Marie. Lilly and Viola Milton knelt staring open-mouthed at the altar. Tony was giggling softly. Only Annie Churchill, her eyes fixed on her Ursuline Manual, was thumping her breast remorsefully, in unison with the priest's "mea maxima culpa." There was something about Annie's attitude of devotion which always gave one a distaste for piety.

Breakfast afforded no opportunity for discussion. At that Spartan meal, French conversation alone was permitted; and even had we been able or willing to employ the hated medium, there was practically no one to talk to. By a triumph of monastic discipline, we were placed at table, at our desks, and at church, next to girls to whom we had nothing to say;—good girls, with medals around their necks, and blue or green ribbons over their shoulders, who served as insulating mediums, as non-conductors, separating us from cheerful currents of speech, and securing, on the whole, a reasonable degree of decorum. I could not open my bursting heart to my neighbours, who sat stolidly consuming bread and butter as though no wild light had dawned upon our horizon. When one of them (she is a nun now) observed painstakingly, "J'espère que nous irons aux bois après midi;" I said "Oui," which was the easiest thing *to* say, and conversation closed at that point. We always did go to the woods on Sunday afternoons, unless it rained. During the week, the big girls—the arrogant and unapproachable First Cours—assumed possession of them as an exclusive right, and left us only Mulberry Avenue in which to play prisoner's base, and Saracens and Crusaders; but on Sundays the situation was reversed, and the Second Cours was led joyously out to those sweet shades which in our childish eyes were vast as Epping Forest, and as full of mystery as the Schwarzwald. No one could have valued this weekly privilege more than I did; but the day was clear, and we were sure to go. I felt the vapid nature of Mary Rawdon's remark to be due solely to the language in which it was uttered. All our inanities were spoken in French; and those nuns who understood no other tongue must have conceived a curious impression of our intelligence.

There was a brief recreation of fifteen minutes at ten o'clock, which sufficed for a rapturous exchange of confidences and speculations. Only those who have been at a convent school can understand how the total absence of man enriches him with a halo of illusion. Here we were, seven absurdly romantic little girls, living in an atmosphere of devout and rarified femininity; and here was a tall Italian youth, at least eighteen, sent by a beneficent Providence to thrill us with emotions. Was he going to stay? we asked with bated breath. Was he going to serve Mass every morning instead of Peter? We could not excite ourselves over Peter, who was a small, freckle-faced country boy, awkwardly shy, and—I should judge—of a saturnine disposition. We had met him once in the avenue, and had asked him if he had any brothers or sisters. "Naw," was the reply. "I had a brother wanst, but he died;—got out of it when he was a baby. He was a cute one, he was." A speech which I can only hope was not so Schopenhauerish as it sounds.

And now, in Peter's place, came this mysterious, dark-eyed, and altogether adorable stranger from beyond the seas. Annie Churchill, who, for all her prayerfulness, had been fully alive to the situation, opined that he was an "exile," and the phrase smote us to the heart. We had read "Elizabeth; or the Exile of Siberia,"—it was in the school library,—and here was a male Elizabeth under our ravished eyes. "That's why he came to a convent," continued Annie, following up her advantage; "to be hidden from all pursuit."

"No doubt he did," said Tony breathlessly, "and we'll have to be very careful not to say anything about him to visitors. We might be the occasion of his being discovered and sent back."

This thought was almost too painful to be borne. Upon our discretion depended perhaps the safety of a heroic youth who had fled from tyranny and cruel injustice. I was about to propose that we should bind ourselves by a solemn vow never to mention his presence, save secretly to one another, when Elizabeth—not the Siberian, but our own unexiled Elizabeth—observed with that biting dryness which was the real secret of her ascendency: "We'd better not say much about him, anyway. On our own account, I mean." Which pregnant remark—the bell for "Christian Instruction" ringing at that moment—sent us silent and meditative to our desks.

So it was that Marianus came to the convent, and we gave him our seven young hearts with unresisting enthusiasm. Viola's heart, indeed, was held of small account, she being only ten years old; but Elizabeth was twelve, and Marie and Annie were thirteen,—ages ripe for passion, and remote from the taunt of immaturity. It was understood from the beginning that we all loved Marianus with equal right and fervour. We shared the emotion fairly and squarely, just as we shared an occasional box of candy, or any other benefaction. It was our common secret,—our fatal secret, we would have said,—and must be guarded with infinite precaution from a cold and possibly disapproving world; but no one of us dreamed of setting up a private romance of her own, of extracting from the situation more than one sixth—leaving Viola out—of its excitement and ecstasy.

We discovered in the course of time our exile's name and nationality,—it was the chaplain who told us,—and also that he was studying for the priesthood; this last information coming from the mistress of recreation, and being plainly designed to dull our interest from the start. She added that he neither spoke nor understood anything but Italian, a statement which we determined to put to the proof as soon as fortune should favour us with the opportunity. The possession of an Italian dictionary became meanwhile imperative, and we had no way of getting such a thing. We couldn't write home for one, because our letters were all read before they were sent out, and any girl would be asked why she had made this singular request. We couldn't beg our mothers, even when we saw them, for dictionaries of a language they knew we were not studying. Lilly said she thought she might ask her father for one, the next time he came to the school. There is a lack of intelligence, or at least of alertness, about fathers, which makes them invaluable in certain emergencies; but which, on the other hand, is apt to precipitate them into blunders. Mr. Milton promised the dictionary, without putting any inconvenient questions, though he must have been a little surprised at the scholarly nature of the request; but just as he was going away, he said loudly and cheerfully:—

"Now what is it I am to bring you next time, children? Mint candy, and handkerchiefs,—your Aunt Helen says you must live on handkerchiefs, —and gloves for Viola, and a dictionary?"

He was actually shaking hands with Madame Bouron, the Mistress General, as he spoke, and she turned to Lilly, and said:—

"Lilly, have you lost your French dictionary, as well as all your handkerchiefs?"

"No, madame," said poor Lilly.

"It's an Italian dictionary she wants this time," corrected Mr. Milton, evidently not understanding why Viola was poking him viciously in the back.

"Lilly is not studying Italian. None of the children are," said Madame Bouron. And then, very slowly, and with an emphasis which made two of her hearers quake: "Lilly has no need of an Italian dictionary, Mr. Milton. She had better devote more time and attention to her French."

"I nearly fainted on the spot," said Lilly, describing the scene to us afterwards; "and father looked scared, and got away as fast as he could;

and Viola was red as a beet; and I thought surely Madame Bouron was going to say something to me; but, thank Heaven! Eloise Didier brought up her aunt to say good-by, and we slipped off. Do you think, girls, she'll ask me what I wanted with an Italian dictionary?"

"Say you're going to translate Dante in the holidays," suggested Tony, with unfeeling vivacity.

"Say you're going to Rome, to see the Pope," said Marie.

"Say you're such an accomplished French scholar, it's time you turned your attention to something else," said Emily.

"Say you're making a collection of dictionaries," said the imp, Viola.

Lilly looked distressed. The humours of the situation were, perhaps, less manifest to her perturbed mind. But Elizabeth, who had been thinking the matter over, observed gloomily: "Oh, Boots" (our opprobrious epithet for the Mistress General) "won't bother to ask questions. She knows all she wants to know. She'll just watch us, and see that we never get a chance to speak to Marianus. It was bad enough before, but it will be worse than ever now. He might almost as well be in Italy."

Things did seem to progress slowly, considering the passionate nature of our devotion. Never was there such an utter absence of opportunity. From the ringing of the first bell at quarter past six in the morning to the lowering of the dormitory lights at nine o'clock at night, we were never alone for a moment, but moved in orderly squadrons through the various duties of the day. Marianus served Mass every morning, and on Sundays assisted at Vespers and Benediction. Outside the chapel, we never saw him. He lived in "Germany,"—a name given, Heaven knows why, to a farm-house on the convent grounds, which was used as quarters for the chaplain and for visitors; but though we cast many a longing look in its direction, no dark Italian head was ever visible at window or at door. I believe my own share of affection was beginning to wither under this persistent blight, when something happened which not only renewed its fervour, but which thrilled my heart with a grateful sentiment, not wholly dead to-day.

It was May,—a month dedicated to the Blessed Virgin, and fuller than usual of church-going, processions, and hymns. We were supposed to be, or at least expected to be, particularly obedient and studious during these four weeks; and, by way of incentive, each class had its candle, tied with the class colour, and standing amid a lovely profusion of spring flowers on the Madonna's altar. There were six of them: white for the graduates, purple for the first class, blue for the second, red for the third, green for the fourth, and pink for the fifth,—the very little girls, for whom the discipline of school life was mercifully relaxed. All the candles were lighted every morning during Mass, unless some erring member of a class had, by misconduct the day before, forfeited the honour, not only for herself, but for her classmates. These tapers were my especial abhorrence. The laudable determination of the third class to keep the red-ribboned candle burning all month maddened me, both by the difficulties it presented, and by the meagre nature of the consequences involved. I could not bring myself to understand why they should care whether it were lit or not. To be sent downstairs to a deserted music-room, there to spend the noon recreation hour in studying Roman history or a French fable;—that was a penalty, hard to avoid, but easy to understand. Common sense and a love of enjoyment made it clear that no one should lightly run such risks. But I had not imagination enough to grasp the importance of a candle more or less upon the altar. It was useless to appeal to my love for the Blessed Virgin. I loved her so well and so confidently, I had placed my childish faith in her so long, that no doubt of her sympathy ever crossed my mind. My own mother might side with authority. Indeed, she represented the supreme, infallible authority, from which there was no appeal. But in every trouble of my poor little gusty life, the Blessed Mother sided with me. Of that, thank Heaven! I felt sure.

This month my path was darkened by a sudden decision on Elizabeth's part that our candle should not be once extinguished. Elizabeth, to do her justice, did not often incline to virtue; but when she did, there was a scant allowance of cakes and ale for any of us. She never deviated from her chosen course, and she never fully understood the sincere but fallible nature of our unkept resolutions. I made my usual frantic, futile effort to follow her lead, with the usual melancholy failure. Before the first week was over, I had come into collision with authority (it was a matter of arithmetic, which always soured my temper to the snapping point); and the sixth of May saw five candles only burning at the veiled Madonna's feet. I sat, angry and miserable, while Madame Duncan, who had charge of the altar, lit the faithful five, and retired with a Rhadamanthine expression to her stall. Elizabeth, at the end of the bench, looked straight ahead, with an expression, or rather an enforced absence of expression, which I perfectly understood. She would not say anything, but none the less would her displeasure be made chillingly manifest. Mass had begun. The priest was reading the Introit, when Marianus lifted a roving eye upon the Blessed Virgin's altar. It was not within his province; he had nothing to do with its flowers or its tapers; but when did generous mind pause for such considerations? He saw that one candle, a candle with a drooping scarlet ribbon, was unlit; and, promptly rising from his knees, he plunged into the sacristy, reappeared with a burning wax-end, and repaired the error, while we held our breaths with agitation and delight. Madame Duncan's head was lowered in seemly prayer; but the ripple of excitement communicated itself mysteriously to her, and she looked up, just as Marianus had deftly accomplished his task. For an instant she half rose to her feet; and then the absurdity of re-attacking the poor little red candle seemed to dawn on her (she was an Irish nun, not destitute of humour), and with a fleeting smile at me,—a smile in which there was as much kindness as amusement,—she resumed her interrupted devotions.

But I tucked my crimson face into my hands, and my soul shouted with joy. Marianus, our idol, our exile, the one true love of our six hearts, had done this deed for me. Not only was I lifted from disgrace, but raised to a preëminence of distinction; for had I not been saved by *him*? Oh, true knight! Oh, chivalrous champion of the unhappy and oppressed! When I recall that moment of triumph, it is even now with a stir of pride, and of something more than pride, for I am grateful still.

That night, that very night, I was just sinking into sleep when a hand was laid cautiously upon my shoulder. I started up. It was too dark to see anything clearly, but I knew that the shadow by my side was Elizabeth. "Come out into the hall," she whispered softly. "You had better creep back of the beds. Don't make any noise!"—and without a sound she was gone.

I slipped on my wrapper,—night-gowns gleam so perilously white,—and with infinite precaution stole behind my sleeping companions, each one curtained safely into her little muslin alcove. At the end of the dormitory I was joined by another silent figure,—it was Marie,—and very gently we pushed open the big doors. The hall outside was flooded with moonlight, and by the open window crouched a bunch of girls, pressed close together,—so close it was hard to disentangle them. A soft gurgle of delight bubbled up from one little throat, and was instantly hushed down by more prudent neighbours. Elizabeth hovered on the outskirts of the group, and, without a word, she pushed me to the sill. Beneath, leaning against a tree, not thirty feet away, stood Marianus. His back was turned to us, and he was smoking. We could see the easy grace of his attitude,—was he not an Italian?—we could smell the intoxicating fragrance of his cigar. Happily unaware of his audience, he smoked, and contemplated the friendly moon, and wondered, perhaps, why the Fates had cast him on this desert island, as remote from human companionship as Crusoe's. Had he known of the six young hearts that had been given him unbidden, it would probably have cheered him less than we imagined.

But to us it seemed as though our shadowy romance had taken form and substance. The graceless daring of Marianus in stationing himself beneath our windows,—or at least beneath a window to which we had possible access; the unholy lateness of the hour,—verging fast upon half-past nine; the seductive moonlight; the ripe profligacy of the cigar;—what was wanting to this night's exquisite adventure! As I knelt breathless in the shadow, my head bobbing against Viola's and Marie's, I thought of Italy, of Venice, of Childe Harold, of everything that was remote, and beautiful, and unconnected with the trammels of arithmetic. I heard Annie Churchill murmur that it was like a serenade; I heard Tony's whispered conjecture as to whether the silent serenader really knew where we slept;—than which nothing seemed less likely;—I heard Elizabeth's warning "Hush!" whenever the muffled voices rose too high above the stillness of the sleeping convent; but nothing woke me from my dreams until Marianus slowly withdrew his shoulder from the supporting tree, and sauntered away, without turning his head once in our direction. We watched him disappear in the darkness; then, closing the window, moved noiselessly back to bed. "Who saw him first?" I asked at the dormitory door.

"I did," whispered Elizabeth; "and I called them all. I didn't intend letting Viola know; but, of course, sleeping next to Lilly, she heard me. She ought to be up in the 'Holy Child' dormitory with the other little girls. It's ridiculous having her following us about everywhere."

And, indeed, Viola's precocious pertinacity made her a difficult problem to solve. There are younger sisters who can be snubbed into impotence. Viola was no such weakling.

But now the story which we thought just begun was drawing swiftly to its close. Perhaps matters had reached a point when something had to happen; yet it did seem strange—it seems strange even now—that the crisis should have been precipitated by a poetic outburst on the part of Elizabeth. Of all the six, she was the least addicted to poetry. She seldom read it, and never spent long hours in copying it in a blank-book, as was our foolish and laborious custom. She hated compositions, and sternly refused the faintest touch of sentiment when compelled to express her thoughts upon "The First Snow-drop," or "My Guardian Angel," or the "Execution of Mary, Queen of Scots." Tony wrote occasional verses of a personal and satiric character, which we held to sparkle with a biting wit. Annie Churchill had once rashly shown to Lilly and to me some feeble lines upon "The Evening Star." Deep hidden in my desk, unseen by mortal eye save mine, lay an impassioned "Soliloquy of Jane Eyre," in blank verse, which was almost volcanic in its fervour, and which perished the following year, unmourned, because unknown to the world. But Elizabeth had never shown the faintest disposition to write anything that could be left unwritten, until Marianus stirred the waters of her soul. That night, that moonlit night, and the dark figure smoking in the shadows, cast their sweet spell upon her. With characteristic promptness, she devoted her French study hour the following afternoon to the composition of a poem, which was completed when we went to class, and which she showed me secretly while we were scribbling our *dictée*. There were five verses, headed "To Marianus," and beginning,—

"Gracefully up the long aisle he glides,"

which was a poetic license, as the chapel aisle was short, and Marianus had never glided up it since he came. He always—in virtue of his office—entered by the sacristy door.

But realism was then as little known in literature as in art, and poetry was not expected to savour of statement rather than emotion. Elizabeth's masterpiece expressed in glowing numbers the wave of sentiment by which we were submerged. Before night it had passed swiftly from hand to hand, and before night the thunderbolt had fallen. Whose rashness was to blame I do not now remember; but, thank Heaven! it was not mine. Some one's giggle was too unsuppressed. Some one thrust the paper too hurriedly into her desk, or dropped it on the floor, or handed it to some one else in a manner too obviously mysterious not to arouse suspicion. I only know that it fell into the hands of little Madame Davide, who had the eyes of a ferret and the heart of a mouse, and who, being unable to read a word of English, sent it forthwith to Madame Bouron. I only know that, after that brief and unsatisfactory glimpse in French class, I never saw it again; which is why I can now recall but one line out of twenty,—a circumstance I devoutly regret.

It was a significant proof of Madame Bouron's astuteness that, without asking any questions, or seeking any further information, she summoned six girls to her study that evening after prayers. She had only the confiscated poem in Elizabeth's writing as a clue to the conspiracy, but she needed nothing more. There we were, all duly indicted, save Viola, whose youth, while it failed to protect us from the unsought privilege of her society, saved her, as a rule, from any retributive measures. Her absence on this occasion was truly a comfort, as her presence would have involved the added and most unmerited reproach of leading a younger child into mischief. Viola was small for her age, and had appealing brown eyes. There was not a nun in the convent who knew her for the imp she was. Lilly, gay, sweet, simple, generous, and unselfish, seemed as wax in her little sister's hands.

There were six of us, then, to bear the burden of blame; and Madame Bouron, sitting erect in the lamplight, apportioned it with an unsparing hand. Her fine face (she was coldly handsome, but we did not like her well enough to know it) expressed contemptuous displeasure; her words conveyed a somewhat exaggerated confidence in our guilt. Of Elizabeth's verses she spoke with icy scorn;—she had not been aware that so gifted a writer graced the school; but the general impropriety of our behaviour was unprecedented in the annals of the convent. That we, members of the Society of St. Aloysius, should have shown ourselves so unworthy of our privileges, and so forgetful of our patron, was a surprise even to her; though (she was frankness itself) she had never entertained a good opinion either of our dispositions or of our intelligence. The result of such misconduct was that the chaplain's assistant must leave at once and forever. Not that *he* had ever wasted a thought upon any girl in the school. His heart was set upon the priesthood. Young though he was, he had already suffered for the Church. His father had fought and died in defence of the Holy See. His home had been lost. He was a stranger in a far land. And now he must be driven from the asylum he had sought, because we could not be trusted to behave with that modesty and discretion which had always been the fairest adornment of children reared within the convent's holy walls. She hoped that we would understand how grievous was the wrong we had done, and that even our callous hearts would bleed when we went to our comfortable beds, and reflected that, because of our wickedness and folly, a friendless and pious young student was once more alone in the world.

It was over! We trailed slowly up to the dormitory, too bewildered to understand the exact nature of our misdoing. The most convincing proof of our mental confusion is that our own immaculate innocence never occurred to any of us. We had looked one night out of the window at Marianus, and Elizabeth had written the five amorous verses. That was all. Not one of us had spoken a word to the object of our affections. Not one of us could boast a single glance, given or received. We had done nothing; yet so engrossing had been the sentiment, so complete the absorption of the past two months, that we, living in a children's world of illusions,—"passionate after dreams, and unconcerned about realities,"—had deemed ourselves players of parts, actors in an unsubstantial drama, intruders into the realms of the forbidden. We accepted this conviction with meekness, untempered by regret; but we permitted ourselves a doubt as to whether our iniquity were wholly responsible for the banishment of Marianus. The too strenuous pointing of a moral breeds skepticism in the youthful soul. When Squire Martin (of our grandfathers' reading-books) assured Billy Freeman that dogs and turkey-cocks were always affable to children who studied their lessons and obeyed their parents, that innocent little boy must have soon discovered for himself that virtue is but a weak bulwark in the barnyard. We, too, had lost implicit confidence in the fine adjustments of life; and, upon this occasion, we found comfort in incredulity. On the stairs Elizabeth remarked to me in a gloomy undertone that Marianus could never have intended to stay at the convent, anyhow, and that he probably had been "sent for." She did not say whence, or by whom; but the mere suggestion was salve to my suffering soul. It enabled me, at least, to bear the sight of Annie Churchill's tears, when, ten minutes later, that weak-minded girl slid into my alcove (as if we were not in trouble enough already), and, sitting forlornly on my bed, asked me in a stifled whisper, "did I think that Marianus was really homeless, and couldn't we make up a sum of money, and send it to him?"

"How much have you got?" I asked her curtly. The complicated emotions through which I had passed had left me in a savage humour; and the peculiar infelicity of this proposal might have irritated St. Aloysius himself. We were not allowed the possession of our own money, though in view of the fact that there was ordinarily nothing to buy with it, extravagance would have been impossible. Every Thursday afternoon the "Bazaar" was opened; our purses, carefully marked with name and number, were handed to us, and we were at liberty to purchase such uninteresting necessities as writing-paper, stamps, blank-books, pencils, and sewing materials. The sole concession to prodigality was a little pile of pious pictures,—small French prints, ornamented with lace paper, which it was our custom to give one another upon birthdays and other festive occasions. They were a great resource in church, where prayer-books, copiously interleaved with these works of art, were passed to and fro for mutual solace and refreshment.

All these things were as well known to Annie as to me, but she was too absorbed in her grief to remember them. She mopped her eyes, and said vacantly that she thought she had a dollar and a half.

"I have seventy-five cents," I said; "and Elizabeth hasn't anything. She spent all her money last Thursday. We might be able to raise five dollars amongst us. If you think that much would be of any use to Marianus, all you have to do is to ask Madame Bouron for our purses, and for his address, and see if she would mind our writing and sending it to him."

Annie, impervious at all times to sarcasm, looked dazed for a moment, her wet blue eyes raised piteously to mine. "Then you think we couldn't manage it?" she asked falteringly.

But I plunged my face into my wash-basin, as a hint that the conversation was at an end. I, too, needed the relief of tears, and was waiting impatiently to be alone.

For Marianus had gone. Of that, at least, there was no shadow of doubt. We should never see him again; and life seemed to stretch before me in endless grey reaches of grammar, and arithmetic, and French conversation; of getting up early in the morning, uncheered by the thought of seeing Marianus serve Mass; of going to bed at night, with never another glance at that dark shadow in the moonlight. I felt that for me the page of love was turned forever, the one romance of my life was past. I cried softly and miserably into my pillow; and resolved, as I did so, that the next morning I would write on the fly-leaves of my new French prayer-book and my "Thomas à Kempis" the lines:—

"'Tis better to have loved and lost,

Than never to have loved at all."

The Convent Stage

"From this hour I do renounce the creed whose fatal worship of bad passions has led thee on, step by step, to this blood-guiltiness!"

Elizabeth was studying her part. We were all studying our parts; but we stopped to listen to this glowing bit of declamation, which Elizabeth delivered with unbroken calm. "I drop down on my knees when I say that," she observed gloomily.

We looked at her with admiring, envious eyes. Our own rôles offered no such golden opportunities. Lilly's, indeed, was almost as easily learned as Snug's, being limited to three words, "The Christian slave?" which were supposed to be spoken interrogatively; but which she invariably pronounced as an abstract statement, bearing on nothing in particular. It was seldom, however, that we insignificant little girls of the Second Cours were permitted to take part in any play, and we felt to the full the honour and glory of our positions. "I come on in three scenes, and speak eleven times," I said, with a pride which I think now strongly resembled Mr. Rushworth's. "What are you, Tony?"

"A beggar child," said Tony. "I cry 'Bread! bread!' in piercing accents" (she was reading from the stage directions), "and afterwards say to Zara, —that's Mary Orr,—'Our thanks are due to thee, noble lady, who from thy abundance feeds us once. Our love and blessings follow her who gave us daily of her slender store.'"

"Is that all?"

"The other beggar child says nothing but 'Bread! bread!'" replied Tony stiffly.

"What a lot of costumes to get up for so many little parts!" commented Elizabeth, ever prone to consider the practical aspect of things.

"I am dressed in rags," said Tony. "They oughtn't to give much trouble."

"Lilly and I are to be dressed alike," I said. "'Slaves of the royal household.' Madame Rayburn said we were to wear Turkish trousers of yellow muslin, with blue tunics, and red sashes tied at the side. Won't we look like guys?"

I spoke with affected disdain and real complacency, gloating—like Mr. Rushworth—over the finery I pretended to despise. Elizabeth stared at us dispassionately. "Lilly will look well in anything," she remarked with disconcerting candour, at which Lilly blushed a lovely rose pink. She knew how pretty she was, but she had that exquisite sweetness of temper which is so natural an accompaniment of beauty. Perhaps we should all be sweet-tempered if we could feel sure that people looked at us with pleasure.

"You will have to wear Turkish trousers, too," said Tony maliciously to Elizabeth; "and get down on your knees in them."

"No, I won't," returned Elizabeth scornfully. "I'm not a Turk. I'm a Moorish princess,—Zara's niece."

"Moors and Turks are the same," said Tony with conviction.

"Moors and Turks are not the same," said Elizabeth. "Turks live in Turkey, and Moors live—Whereabouts is this play, anyway, Marie?"

"Granada," said Marie. "The Spanish army, under Ferdinand and Isabella, is besieging Granada. I wish I were a Moor instead of a pious Spanish lady. It would be a great deal more fun. I've always got pious parts."

This was true, but then most of the parts in our convent plays *were* pious, and if they were given to Marie, it was because she was so good an actress,—the only one our Second Cours could boast. Elizabeth, indeed, had her merits. She never forgot her lines, never was frightened, never blundered. But her absolutely unemotional rendering of the most heroic sentiments chilled her hearers' hearts. Marie was fervid and impassioned. Her *r-r*'s had the true Gallic roll. Her voice vibrated feelingly. She was tall for thirteen, without being hopelessly overgrown as Emily and I were. Strangest of all, she did not seem to mind the foolish and embarrassing things which she was obliged to do upon the stage. She would fling her arms around an aged parent, and embrace her fondly. She would expound the truths of Christianity, as St. Philomena. She would weep, and pray, and forgive her enemies, as the luckless Madame Elisabeth. What is more, she would do these things at rehearsals, in her short school frock, with unabated fervour, and without a shade of embarrassment. We recognized her as a Heaven-sent genius, second only to Julia Reynolds and Antoinette Mayo (who I still think *must* have been the greatest of living actresses), yet in our secret souls we despised a little such absolute lack of self-consciousness. We were so awkward and abashed when brought face to face with any emotion, so incapable of giving it even a strangled utterance, that Marie's absorption in her parts seemed to us a trifle indecent. It was on a par with her rapid French, her lively gestures, her openly expressed affection for the nuns she liked, and the unconcern with which she would walk up the long classroom, between two rows of motionless girls, to have a medal hung around her neck on Sunday night at Primes. This hideous ordeal, which clouded our young lives, was no more to Marie than walking upstairs,—no more than unctuously repeating every day for a fortnight the edifying remarks of the pious Spanish lady.

Plays were the great diversions of our school life. We had two or three of them every winter, presented, it seemed to me, with dazzling splendour, and acted with passionate fire. I looked forward to these performances with joyful excitement, I listened, steeped in delight, I dreamed of them afterwards for weeks. The big girls who played in them, and of whom I knew little but their names, were to me beings of a remote and exalted nature. The dramas themselves were composed with a view to our especial needs, or rather to our especial limitations. Their salient feature was the absence of courtship and of love. It was part of the convent system to ignore the master passion, to assume that it did not exist, to banish from our work and from our play any reference to the power that moves the world. The histories we studied skipped chastely on from reign to reign, keeping always at bay this riotous intruder. The books we read were as free as possible from any taint of infection. The poems we recited were as serene and cold as Teneriffe. "Love in the drama," says an acrimonious critic, "plays rather a heavy part." It played no part at all in ours, and I am disposed to look back now upon its enforced absence as an agreeable elimination. The students of St. Omer—so I have been told—presented a French version of "Romeo and Juliet," with all the love scenes left out. This *tour de force* was beyond our scope; but "She Stoops to Conquer," shorn of its double courtship, made a vivacious bit of comedy, and a translation of "Le Malade Imaginaire"—expurgated to attenuation—was the most successful farce of the season.

Of course the expurgation was not done by us. We knew Goldsmith and Molière only in their convent setting, where, it is safe to say, they would never have known themselves. Most of our plays, however, were original productions, written by some one of the nuns whose talents chanced to be of a dramatic order. They were, as a rule, tragic in character, and devout in sentiment,—sometimes so exceedingly devout as to resemble religious homilies rather than the legitimate drama. A conversation held in Purgatory, which gave to three imprisoned souls an opportunity to tell one another at great length, and with shameless egotism, the faults and failings of their lives, was not—to our way of thinking—a play. We listened unmoved to the disclosures of these garrulous spirits, who had not sinned deeply enough to make their revelations interesting. It was like going to confession on a large and liberal scale. The martyrdom of St. Philomena was nearly as dull, though the saint's defiance of the tyrant Symphronius—"persecutor of the innocent, slayer of the righteous, despot whose knell has even this hour rung"—lent a transient gleam of emotion; and the angel who visited her in prison—and who had great difficulty getting his wings through the narrow prison door—was, to my eyes at least, a vision of celestial beauty.

What we really loved were historical dramas, full of great names and affecting incidents. Our crowning triumph (several times repeated) was "Zuma," a Peruvian play in which an Indian girl is accused of poisoning the wife of the Spanish general, when she is really trying to cure her of a fever by giving her quinine, a drug known only to the Peruvians, and the secret of which the young captive has sworn never to divulge. "Zuma" was a glorious play. Its first production marked an epoch in our lives. Gladly would we have given it a season's run, had such indulgence been a possibility. There was one scene between the heroine and her free and unregenerate sister, Italca, which left an indelible impression upon my mind. It took place in a subterranean cavern. The stage was darkened, and far-off music—the sound of Spanish revelry—floated on the air. Italca brings Zuma a portion of bark, sufficient only for her own needs, —for she too is fever-stricken,—but, before giving it, asks with piercing scorn: "Are you still an Inca's daughter, or a Castilian slave?"—a question at which poor Zuma can only weep piteously, but which sent thrills of rapture down my youthful spine. I have had my moments of emotion since then. When Madame Bernhardt as La Tosca put the lighted candles on either side of the murdered Scarpia, and laid the crucifix upon his breast. When Madame Duse as Magda turned suddenly upon the sleek Von Keller, and for one awful moment loosened the floodgates of her passion and her scorn: "You have asked after Emma and after Katie. You have not asked for your child." But never again has my soul gone out in such a tumult of ecstasy as when Zuma and Italca, Christian and Pagan sisters, the captive and the unconquered, faced each other upon our convent stage.

And now for the first time I—I, eleven years old, and with no shadowy claim to distinction—was going to take part in a play, was going to tread the boards in yellow Turkish trousers, and speak eleven times for all the school to hear. No fear of failure, no reasonable misgivings fretted my heart's content. Marie might scorn the Spanish lady's rôle; but then Marie had played "Zuma,"—had reached at a bound the highest pinnacle of fame. Elizabeth might grumble at giving up our recreation hours to rehearsals; but then Elizabeth had been one of the souls in Purgatory, the sinfullest soul, and the most voluble of all. Besides, nothing ever elated Elizabeth. She had been selected once to make an address to the Archbishop, and to offer him a basket of flowers; he had inquired her name, and had said he knew her father; yet all this public notice begot in her no arrogance of soul. Her only recorded observation was to the effect that, if she were an archbishop, she wouldn't listen to addresses; a suggestion which might have moved the weary and patient prelate more than did the ornate assurances of our regard.

With this shining example of insensibility before my eyes, I tried hard to conceal my own inordinate pride. Rehearsals began before we knew our parts, and the all-important matter of costumes came at once under consideration. The "play-closet," that mysterious receptacle of odds and ends, of frayed satins, pasteboard swords, and tarnished tinsel jewelry, was soon exhausted of its treasures. Some of the bigger girls, who were to be Spanish ladies in attendance upon Queen Isabella, persuaded their mothers to lend them old evening gowns. The rest of the clothes we manufactured ourselves, "by the pure light of reason," having no models of any kind to assist or to disturb us.

Happily, there were no Spanish men in the play. Men always gave a good deal of trouble, because they might not, under any circumstances, be clad in male attire. A short skirt, reaching to the knee, and generally made of a balmoral petticoat, was the nearest compromise permitted. Marlow, that consummate dandy, wore, I remember, a red and black striped skirt, rubber boots, a black jacket, a high white collar, and a red cravat. The cravat was given to Julia Reynolds, who played the part, by her brother. It indicated Marlow's sex, and was considered a little indecorous in its extreme mannishness. "They'll hardly know what she" (Mrs. Potts) "is meant for, will they?" asks Mr. Snodgrass anxiously, when that estimable lady proposes going to Mrs. Leo Hunter's fancy ball as Apollo, in a white satin gown with spangles. To which Mr. Winkle makes indignant answer: "Of course they will. They'll see her lyre." With the same admirable acumen, we who saw Marlow's cravat recognized him immediately as a man.

Moors, and Peruvians, and ancient Romans were more easily attired. They wore skirts as a matter of course, looked a good deal alike, and resembled in the main the "Two Gentlemen of Verona," as costumed by Mr. Abbey. It is with much pleasure I observe how closely—if how unconsciously—Mr. Abbey has followed our convent models. His Valentine might be Manco or Cléante strutting upon our school stage. His Titania is a white-veiled first communicant.

The Turkish trousers worn by Lilly and by me—also by Elizabeth, to her unutterable disgust—were allowed because they were portions of feminine attire. Made of rattling paper muslin, stiff, baggy, and with a hideous tendency to slip down at every step, they evoked the ribald mirth of all the other actors. Mary Orr, especially, having firmly declined a pair as part of Zara's costume, was moved to such unfeeling laughter at the first dress rehearsal that I could hardly summon courage to stand by Lilly's side. "The more you show people you mind a thing, the more they'll do it;" Elizabeth had once observed out of the profundity of her school experience,—an experience which dated from her seventh year. Her own armour of assumed unconcern was provocation-proof. She had mistrusted the trousers from the beginning, while I, thinking of Lalla Rookh and Nourmahal (ladies unknown to the convent library), had exulted in their opulent Orientalism. She had expressed dark doubts as to their fit and shape; and had put them on with visible reluctance, and only because no choice had been allowed her. The big girls arranged—within limits—their own costumes, but the little girls wore what was given them. Yet the impenetrable calm with which she presented herself dulled the shafts of schoolgirl sarcasm. You might as well have tried to cauterize a wooden leg—to use Mirabeau's famous simile—as to have tried to provoke Elizabeth.

"Isabella of Castile" was a tragedy. Its heroine, Inez, was held a captive by the Moors, and was occupying herself when the play opened with the conversion to Christianity of Ayesha, the assumed daughter of the ever-famous Hiaya Alnayar,—a splendid anachronism (at the siege of Granada), worthy of M. Sardou. Inez embodied all the Christian virtues, as presented only too often for our consideration. She was so very good that she could hardly help suspecting how good she was; and she never spoke without uttering sentiments so noble and exalted that the Moors—simple children of nature—hated her unaffectedly, and made life as disagreeable for her as they knew how. The powers of evil were represented by Zara, sister of Hiaya, and the ruling spirit of Granada. Enlightened criticism would now call Zara a patriot; but we held sterner views. It was she who defied the Spaniards, who refused surrender, and who, when hope had fled, plotted the murder of Isabella. It was she who persecuted the saintly Inez, and whose dagger pierced Ayesha's heart in the last tumultuous scene. A delightful part to act! I knew every line of it before the rehearsals were over, and I used to rant through it in imagination when I was supposed to be studying my lessons, and when I was lying in my little bed. There were glowing moments when I pictured to myself Mary Orr falling ill the very day of the performance, Madame Rayburn in despair, everybody thunderstruck and helpless, and I stepping modestly forward to confess I knew the part. I saw myself suddenly the centre of attention, the forlorn hope of a desperate emergency, my own insignificant speeches handed over to any one who could learn them, and I storming through Zara's lines to the admiration and wonder of the school. The ease with which I sacrificed Mary Orr to this ambitious vision is pleasing now to contemplate; but I believe I should have welcomed the Bubonic plague, with the prospect of falling its victim the next day, to have realized my dreams.

"One crowded hour of glorious life

Is worth an age without a name."

It was a pity that none of this dramatic fervour found expression in my own rôle, which, though modest, was not without its possibilities. But I was ardent only in imagination, dramatic only in my dreams. When it came to words, I was tame and halting; when it came to gestures, I was awkward and constrained. In vain Madame Rayburn read and re-read me my lines, which, in her clear, flexible voice, took on meaning and purpose. In vain she sought to impress upon me my own especial characteristics,—a slavish spitefulness and servility. It was my privilege to appear in the first scene, and to make the first speech of any importance,—to strike, as I was told, the keynote of the play. The rising curtain revealed Ayesha (Julia Reynolds) in her father's palace; Lilly and I in attendance.

Ayesha. Send hither Inez.

Lilly. (Her one great effort.) The Christian slave?

Ayesha (impatiently). Is there another Inez in the household? You may both retire.

Obediently we bowed and retired; but on the threshold I remarked to Lilly in a bitter undertone, audible only to the house: "Ay! ay, we may retire. And yet I think her noble kinsmen would deem our songs and tales better amusement for a winter's eve than all these whispered controversies on the Christian faith that last sometimes the whole night through. I've overheard them. But wait until Zara returns."

"Try and say those last words threateningly," Madame Rayburn would entreat. "Remember you are going to betray Ayesha's secret. '*Wait* until Zara returns.' And you might clench your right hand. Your *right* hand. No, no, don't raise it. Julia, if you giggle so, I shall never be able to teach the children anything. You embarrass and confuse them. Try once more: '*Wait* until Zara returns.' Now enter Inez. 'Lady, you sent for me.'"

Rehearsals were, on the whole, not an unmixed delight. A large circle of amused critics is hardly conducive to ease, and the free expression of dramatic force,—at least, not when one is eleven years old, and painfully shy. I envied Marie her fervour and pathos, her clasped hands and uplifted eyes. I envied Elizabeth her business-like repose, the steady, if somewhat perfunctory, fashion in which she played her part. I envied Lilly, who halted and stammered over her three words, but whose beauty made amends for all shortcomings. Yet day by day I listened with unabated interest to the familiar lines. Day by day the climax awoke in me the same sentiments of pity and exultation. Moreover, the distinction of being in the cast was something solid and satisfactory. It lifted me well above the heads of less fortunate, though certainly not less deserving, classmates. It enabled me to assume an attitude toward Annie Churchill and Emily which I can only hope they were generous enough to forgive. It was an honour universally coveted, and worth its heavy cost.

The night came. The stage was erected at one end of our big study-room (classic-hall, we called it); the audience, consisting of the school and the nuns, for no strangers were admitted on these occasions, sat in serried ranks to witness our performance. Behind the scenes, despite the frenzy of suppressed excitement, there reigned outward order and tranquillity. The splendid precision of our convent training held good in all emergencies. We revolved like spheres in our appointed orbits, and confusion was foreign to our experience. I am inclined to think that the habit of self-restraint induced by this gentle inflexibility of discipline, this exquisite sense of method and proportion, was the most valuable by-product of our education. There was an element of dignity in being even an insignificant part of a harmonious whole.

At the stroke of eight the curtain rose. Ayesha, reclining upon cushions, and wearing all the chains and necklaces the school could boast, listens with rapture to the edifying discourse of Inez, and confesses her readiness to be baptized. Inez gives pious thanks for this conversion, not forgetting to remind the Heavenly powers that it was through her agency it was effected. Into this familiar atmosphere of controversy the sudden return of Zara brings a welcome breath of wickedness and high resolve. Granada is doomed. Her days are numbered. The Spanish army, encamped in splendour, awaits her inevitable fall. Her ruler is weak and vacillating. Her people cry for bread. But Zara's spirit is unbroken. She finds Inez—in whom every virtue and every grace conspire to exasperate—distributing her own portion of food to clamorous beggars, and sweeps her sternly aside: "Dare not again degrade a freeborn Moslem into a recipient of thy Christian charity." She vows that if the city cannot be saved, its fall shall be avenged, and that the proud Queen of Castile shall never enter its gates in triumph.

Dark whispers of assassination fill the air. The plot is touching in its simplicity. Inez, a captive of rank, is to be sent as a peace offering to the Spanish lines. Ayesha and Zoraiya (Elizabeth) accompany her as pledges of good faith. Zara, disguised as a serving woman, goes with them,—her soul inflamed with hate, her dagger hidden in her breast. Ayesha is kept in ignorance of the conspiracy; but Zoraiya knows,—knows that the queen is to be murdered, and that her own life will help to pay the penalty. "Does she consent?" whispers a slave to me; to which I proudly answer: "Consent! Ay, gladly. If it be well for Granada that this Spanish queen should die, then Zara's niece, being of Zara's blood, thinks neither of pity nor precaution. She says she deals with the Castilian's life as with her own, and both are forfeited."

The scene shifts—by the help of our imagination, for scene-shifters we had none—to Santa Fe, that marvellous camp, more like a city than a battlefield, where the Spaniards lie entrenched. It is an hour of triumph for Inez, and, as might be expected, she bears herself with superlative and maddening sanctity. She is all the Cardinal Virtues rolled into one.

To live with the Saints in Heaven

Is untold bliss and glory;

But to live with the saints on earth

Is quite another story.

When I—meanly currying favour—beg her to remember that I have ever stood her friend, she replies with proud humility: "I will remember naught that I have seen, or heard, or suffered in Granada; and therein lies your safety."

The rôle of Isabella of Castile was played by Frances Fenton, a large, fair girl, with a round face, a slow voice, and an enviable placidity of disposition; a girl habitually decorated with all the medals, ribbons, and medallions that the school could bestow for untarnished propriety of behaviour. She wore a white frock of noticeable simplicity ("so great a soul as Isabella," said Madame Rayburn, "could never stoop to vanity"), a blue sash, and a gold crown, which was one of our most valued stage properties. Foremost among the ladies who surrounded her was Marie, otherwise the Marchioness de Moya, mother of Inez, and also—though this has still to be divulged—of the long-lost Ayesha. It is while the marchioness is clasping Inez in her maternal arms, and murmuring thanks to Heaven, and all the other Spanish ladies are clasping their hands, and murmuring thanks to Heaven, that Zara sees her opportunity to stab the unsuspecting queen. She steals cautiously forward (my throbbing heart stood still), and draws the dagger—a mother-of-pearl paper knife—from the folds of her dress. But Ayesha, rendered suspicious by conversion, is watching her closely. Suddenly she divines her purpose, and, when Zara's arm is raised to strike, she springs forward to avert the blow. It pierces her heart, and with a gasp she falls dying at Isabella's feet.

Every word that followed is engraven indelibly upon my memory. I have forgotten much since then, but only with death can this last scene be effaced from my recollection. It was now that Elizabeth was to make her vehement recantation, was to be converted with Shakespearian speed. It was now she was to fall upon her knees, and abjure Mohammedanism forever. She did not fall. She took a step forward, and knelt quietly and decorously by Ayesha's side, as if for night prayers. Her volcanic language contrasted strangely with the imperturbable tranquillity of her demeanour.

Zoraiya. Oh! Zara, thou hast slain her, slain the fair flower of Granada. The darling of Hiaya's heart is dead.

Spanish Lady. The girl speaks truth. 'Twas Zara's arm that struck.

Zoraiya (conscientiously). From this hour I do renounce the creed whose fatal worship of bad passions has led thee on, step by step, to this blood-guiltiness.

Zara. Peace, peace, Zoraiya! Degrade not thyself thus for one not of thy blood nor race.

Zoraiya. Thy brother's child not of our blood nor race! Thy crime has made thee mad.

Zara. Thou shalt see. I would have word with the Marchioness de Moya.

Marchioness de Moya (springing forward). Why namest thou me, woman? O Queen! why does this Moslem woman call on me?

Isabella (with uplifted eyes). Pray, pray! my friend. Naught else can help thee in this hour which I see coming. For, oh! this is Heaven-ordained.

Zara. Thou hadst a daughter?

Marchioness de Moya. I have one.

Zara. One lost to thee in infancy, when Hiaya stormed Alhama. If thou wouldst once again embrace her, take in thine arms thy dying child.

Marchioness de Moya (unsteadily). Thy hatred to our race is not unknown. Thou sayest this, seeking to torture me. But know, 'twere not torture, 'twere happiness, to believe thy words were words of truth.

Zara. I would not make a Christian happy. But the words are spoken, and cannot be withdrawn. For the rest, Hiaya, whose degenerate wife reared as her own the captive child, will not dispute its truth, now that she is passing equally away from him and thee.

Spanish Lady. Oh! hapless mother!

Marchioness de Moya (proudly). Hapless! I would not change my dying child for any living one in Christendom.

And now, alas! that I must tell it, came the burning humiliation of my childhood. Until this moment, as the reader may have noticed, no one had offered to arrest Zara, nor staunch Ayesha's wound, nor call for aid, nor do any of the things that would naturally have been done off the stage. The necessity of explaining the situation had overridden—as it always does in the drama—every other consideration. But now, while the queen was busy embracing the marchioness, and while the Spanish ladies were bending over Ayesha's body, it was my part to pluck Zara's robe, and whisper: "Quick, quick, let us be gone! To linger here is death." To which she scornfully retorts: "They have no thought of thee, slave; and, as for me, I go to meet what fate Allah ordains:" and slowly leaves the stage.

But where *was* I? Not in our convent schoolroom, not on our convent stage; but in the queen's pavilion, witness to a tragedy which rent my soul in twain. Ayesha (I had a passionate admiration for Julia Reynolds), lying dead and lovely at my feet; Marie's pitiful cry vibrating in my ears; and Zara's splendid scorn and hatred overriding all pity and compunction. Wrapped in the contemplation of these things, I stood speechless and motionless, oblivious of cues, unaware of Zara's meaning glance, unconscious of the long, strained pause, or of Madame Rayburn's loud prompting from behind the scenes. At last, hopeless of any help in my direction, Zara bethought herself to say: "As for me, I go to meet what fate Allah ordains:" and stalked off,—which independent action brought me to my senses with a start. I opened my mouth to speak, but it was too late; and, realizing the horror of my position, I turned and fled,—fled to meet the flood-tide of Mary Orr's reproaches.

"Every one will think that I forgot my lines," she stormed. "Didn't you see me looking straight at you, and waiting for my cue? The whole scene was spoiled by your stupidity."

I glanced miserably at Madame Rayburn. Of all the nuns I loved her best; but I knew her too well to expect any comfort from her lips. Her brown eyes were very cold and bright. "The scene was not spoiled," she said judicially; "it went off remarkably well. But I did think, Agnes, that, although you cannot act, you had too much interest in the play, and too much feeling for the situation, to forget entirely where you were, or what you were about. There, don't cry! It didn't matter much."

Don't cry! As well say to the pent-up dam, "Don't overflow!" or to the heaving lava-bed, "Don't leave your comfortable crater!" Already my tears were raining down over my blue tunic and yellow trousers. How could I—poor, inarticulate child—explain that it was because of my absorbing interest in the play, my passionate feeling for the situation, that I was now humbled to the dust, and that my career as an actress was closed?

In Retreat

WE were on the eve of a "spiritual retreat,"—four whole days of silence, —and, in consideration of this fact, were enjoying the unusual indulgence of an hour's recreation after supper. The gravity of the impending change disturbed our spirits, and took away from us—such is the irony of fate—all desire to talk. We were not precisely depressed, although four days of silence, of sermons, of "religious exercises," and examinations of conscience, might seem reasonably depressing. But on the other hand,—happy adjustment of life's burdens,—we should have no lessons to study, no dictations to write, no loathsome arithmetic to fret our peaceful hearts. The absence of French for four whole days was, in itself, enough to sweeten the pious prospect ahead of us. Elizabeth firmly maintained she liked making retreats; but then Elizabeth regarded her soul's perils with a less lively concern than I did. She was not cursed with a speculative temperament.

What we all felt, sitting silent and somewhat apprehensive in the lamplight, was a desire to do something outrageous,—something which should justify the plunge we were about to make into penitence and compunction of heart. It was the stirring of the Carnival spirit within us, the same intensely human impulse which makes the excesses of Shrove Tuesday a prelude to the first solemn services of Lent. The trouble with us was that we did not know what to do. Our range of possible iniquities was at all times painfully limited. When I recall it, I am fain to think of a pleasant conceit I once heard from Mr. Royce, concerning the innocence of baby imps. Thanks to the closeness of our guardianship, and to the pure air we breathed, no little circle of azure-winged cherubim were ever more innocent than we; yet there were impish promptings in every guiltless heart. Is it possible to look at those cheerful, snub-nosed angels that circle around Fra Lippo Lippi's madonnas, without speculating upon the superfluity of naughtiness that must be forgiven them day by day?

"We might blow out the lights," suggested Lilly feebly.

Elizabeth shook her head, and the rest of us offered no response. To blow out the schoolroom lamps was one of those heroic misdeeds which could be attempted only in moments of supreme excitement, when some breathless romping game had raised our spirits to fever pitch. It was utterly out of keeping with our present mood, and besides it was not really wrong,—only forbidden under penalties. We were subtle enough

—at least some of us were; nobody expected subtlety from Lilly—to recognize the difference.

A silence followed. Tony's chin was sunk in the palm of her hand. When she lifted her head, her brown eyes shone with a flickering light. An enchanting smile curved her crooked little mouth. "Let's steal the straws from under the Bambino in the corridor," she said.

We rose swiftly and simultaneously to our feet. Here was a crime, indeed; a crime which offered the twofold stimulus of pillage and impiety. The Bambino, a little waxen image we all ardently admired, reposed under a glass case in the wide hall leading to the chapel. He lay with his dimpled arms outstretched on a bed of symmetrically arranged straws; not the common, fuzzy, barnyard straws, but these large, smooth cylinders, through which all children love to suck up lemonade and soda water. Soda water was to us an unknown beverage, and lemonade the rarest of indulgences; but we had always coveted the straws, though the unblessed thought of taking them had never entered any mind before. Now, welcoming the temptation, and adding deceit to all the other sins involved, we put on our black veils, and made demure pretence of going to the chapel to pray. Except to go to the chapel, five little girls would never have been permitted to leave the schoolroom together; and, under ordinary circumstances, this sudden access of piety might have awakened reasonable suspicions in the breast of the Mistress of recreation. But the impending retreat made it seem all right to her (she was no great student of human nature), and her friendly smile, as we curtsied and withdrew, brought a faint throb of shame to my perfidious soul.

Once outside the door, we scuttled swiftly to the chapel hall. It was silent and empty. Tony lifted the heavy glass cover which protected the Bambino,—the pretty, helpless baby we were going to ruthlessly rob. For a moment my inborn reverence conquered, and I stooped to kiss the waxen feet. Then, surging hotly through my heart, came the thought,—a Judas kiss; and with a shudder I pulled myself away. By this time, I didn't want the straws, I didn't want to take them at all; but, when one sins in company, one must respect one's criminal obligations. "Honour among thieves." Hurriedly we collected our spoils,—ten shining tubes, which left horrid gaps in the Bambino's bed. Then the case was lowered, and we stood giggling and whispering in the corridor.

"Let's"—said Tony.

But what new villainy she meditated, we never knew. The chapel door opened,—it was Madame Bouron,—and we fled precipitately back to the schoolroom. As we reached it, the clanging of a bell struck dolorously upon our ears. Our last free hour was over, and silence, the unbroken silence of four days, had fallen like a pall upon the convent. We took off our veils, and slipped limply into line for prayers.

The next morning a new order of things reigned throughout the hushed school. The French conversation, which ordinarily made pretence of enlivening our breakfast hour, was exchanged for a soothing stillness. In place of our English classes, we had a sermon from Father Santarius, some chapters of religious reading, and a quiet hour to devote to any pious exercise we deemed most profitable to our souls. Dinner and supper were always silent meals, and one of the older girls read aloud to us,—a pleasant and profitable custom. Now the travels of Père Huc—a most engaging book—was laid aside in favour of Montalembert's "Life of St. Elizabeth of Hungary,"—which also had its charm. Many deficiencies there were in our educational scheme,—it was so long ago, —but the unpardonable sin of commonplaceness could never be counted its shortcoming. After dinner there was an "instruction" from one of the nuns, and more time for private devotions. Then came our three-o'clock *goûter*, followed by a second instruction, Benediction, and the Rosary. After supper, Father Santarius preached to us again in the dimly lit chapel, and our fagged little souls were once more forcibly aroused to the contemplation of their imminent peril. Death, Judgment, Hell, and Heaven—which the catechism says are "the four last things to be remembered"—were the subjects of the four night sermons. Those were not days when soothing syrup was administered in tranquillizing doses from the pulpit.

A sense of mystery attached itself to Father Santarius, attributable, I think, to his immense size, which must have equalled that of St. Thomas

Aquinas. It was said that he had not seen his own feet for twenty years (so vast a bulk intervened), and this interesting legend was a source of endless speculation to little, lean, elastic girls. He was an eloquent and dramatic preacher, versed in all the arts of oratory, and presenting a striking contrast to our dull and gentle chaplain, one of the kindest and most colourless of men, to whose sermons we had long ceased to listen very attentively. We listened to Father Santarius, listened trembling while he thundered his denunciations against worldliness, and infidelity, and pride of place, and many dreadful sins we stood in no immediate danger of committing. The terrors of the Judgment Day were unfurled before our startled eyes with the sympathetic appreciation of a fifteenth-century fresco, and the dead weight of eternity oppressed our infant souls. Father Santarius knew his Hell as well as did Dante, and his Heaven (but we had not yet come to Heaven) a great deal better. Moreover, while Dante's Hell was arranged for the accommodation of those whom he was pleased to put in it, Father Santarius's Hell was prepared for the possible accommodation of *us*,—which made a vast difference in our philosophy. Perhaps a similar sense of liability might have softened the poet's vision. The third night's sermon reduced Annie Churchill to hysterical sobs; Marie was very white, and Elizabeth looked grave and uncomfortable. As for me, my troubled heart must have found expression in my troubled eyes, when I raised them to Madame Rayburn's face as we filed out of the chapel. She was not given to caresses, but she laid her hand gently on my black-veiled head. "Not for you, Agnes," she said, "not for you. Don't be fearful, child!" thus undoing in one glad instant the results of an hour's hard preaching, and sending me comforted to bed.

The next afternoon I was seated at my desk in the interval between an instruction on "human respect"—which we accounted a heavy failing—and Benediction. We were all of us to go to confession on the following day; and, by way of preparation for this ordeal, I was laboriously examining my conscience, and writing down a list of searching questions, which were supposed to lay bare the hidden iniquities of my life, and to pave the way to those austere heights of virtue I hopefully expected to climb. It was a lengthy process, and threatened to consume most of the afternoon.

"Is my conversation always charitable and edifying?"

"Do I pride myself upon my talents and accomplishments?"

"Have I freed my heart from all inordinate affection for created things?"

"Do I render virtue attractive and pleasing to those who differ from me in religion?"—I wrote slowly in my little, cramped, legible hand.

At this point Elizabeth crossed the schoolroom, and touched me on the shoulder. She carried her coral rosary, which she dangled before my eyes for a minute, and then pointed to the door, an impressive dumb show which meant that we should go somewhere, and say our beads together. There were times when the sign language we used in retreat became as animated as conversation, and a great deal more distracting, because of the difficulty we had in understanding it; but the discipline of those four days demanded above all things that we should not speak an unnecessary word. We became fairly skilled in pantomime by the time the days were over.

On the present occasion, Elizabeth's rosary gave its own message, and I alacritously abandoned my half-tilled conscience for this new field of devotion. We meant to walk up and down the chapel hall (past the despoiled Bambino), but at the schoolroom door we encountered Madame Rayburn.

"Where are you going, children?" she asked.

This being an occasion for articulate speech, Elizabeth replied that we were on our way to the corridor to say our beads.

"You had better be out of doors," Madame Rayburn said. "You look as if you needed fresh air. Go into the avenue until the bell rings for Benediction. No farther, remember, or you may be late. You had better take your veils with you to save time."

This *was* being treated with distinction. Sent out of doors by ourselves, just as if we were First Cours girls,—those privileged creatures whom we had seen for the last three days pacing gravely and silently up and down the pleasant walks. No such liberty had ever been accorded to us before, and I felt a thrill of pride when Julia Reynolds—walking alone in the avenue—raised her eyes from the "Pensées Chrétiennes" of Madame Swetchine (I recognized its crimson cover, having been recently obliged to translate three whole pages of it as a penance), and stared at us with the abstract impersonal gaze of one engrossed in high spiritual concerns. It was a grey day in early June, a soft and windless day, and, as we walked sedately under the big mulberry trees, a sense of exquisite well-being stole into my heart. I was conscious of some faint appreciation of the tranquillity that breathed around me, some dim groping after the mystery of holiness, some recognizable content in the close companionship of my friend. I forgot that I was going to free myself from all inordinate affection for created things, and knew only that it was pleasant to walk by Elizabeth's side.

"Let us contemplate in this second joyful mystery the visitation of the Blessed Virgin Mary to her cousin, St. Elizabeth," she said.

Why, there it was! The Blessed Virgin's cousin was named Elizabeth, too. Of course they were friends; perhaps they were very fond of each other; only St. Elizabeth was so much too old. Could one have a real friend, years older than one's self? My mind was wandering over this aspect of the case while I pattered my responses, and my pearl beads—not half so pretty as Elizabeth's coral ones—slipped quickly through my fingers. When we had finished the five decades, and had said the *De profundis* for the dead, there was still time on our hands. The chapel bell had not yet rung. We walked for a few minutes in silence, and then I held up my rosary as a suggestion that we should begin the sorrowful mysteries. But Elizabeth shook her head.

"Let's have a little serious conversation," she said.

Not Balaam, when he heard the remonstrance of his ass, not Albertus Magnus, when the brazen head first opened its lips and spoke, was more startled and discomfited than I. Such a proposal shook my moral sense to its foundations. But Elizabeth's light blue eyes—curiously light, by contrast with her dark skin and hair—were raised to mine with perfect candour and good faith. It was plain that she did not hold herself a temptress.

"A little *serious* conversation," she repeated with emphasis.

For a moment I hesitated. Three speechless days made the suggestion a very agreeable one, and I was in the habit of consenting to whatever Elizabeth proposed. But conversation, even serious conversation, was a daring innovation for a retreat, and I was not by nature an innovator. Then suddenly a happy thought came to me. I had brought along my Ursuline Manual (in those days we went about armed with all our spiritual weapons), and I opened it at a familiar page.

"Let's find out our predominant passions," I said.

Elizabeth consented joyfully. Her own prayer-book was French, a *Paroissien Romain*, and the predominant passions had no place in it. She was evidently flattered by the magnificence of the term, as applied to her modest transgressions. It was something to know—at twelve—that one was possessed of a passion to predominate.

"We'll skip the advice in the beginning?" she said.

I nodded, and Elizabeth, plunging, as was her wont, into the heart of the matter, read with impressive solemnity:—

"The predominant passion of many young people is pride, which never fails to produce such haughtiness of manner and self-sufficiency as to render them equally odious and ridiculous. Incessantly endeavouring to attract admiration, and become the sole objects of attention, they spare no pains to set themselves off, and to outdo their companions. By their conceited airs, their forwardness, their confidence in their own opinions, and neglect or contempt of that timid, gentle, retiring manner, so amiable and attractive in youth, they defeat their own purpose, and become as contemptible as they aim at being important."

There was a pause. The description sounded so little like either of us that I expected Elizabeth to go right on to more promising vices. But she was evidently turning the matter over in her mind.

"I think that's Adelaide Harrison's predominant passion," she said at length.

Somewhat surprised, I acquiesced. It had not occurred to me to send my thoughts wandering over the rest of the school, or I should, perhaps, have reached some similar conclusion.

"Yes, it's certainly Adelaide Harrison's passion," Elizabeth went on thoughtfully. "You remember how she behaved about that composition of hers, 'The Woods in Autumn,' that Madame Duncan thought so fine. She said she ought to be able to write a good composition when her mother had written a whole volume of poems, and her brother had written something else,—I don't remember what. That's what *I* call pride."

"She says they are a talented family," I added maliciously. ("Is my conversation always charitable and edifying?") "That she taught herself to read when she was six years old, and that they all speak French when they are together. I don't believe that."

"It must be horrid, if they do," said Elizabeth. "I'm glad I'm not one of them. Vous ne mangez rien, ma chère Adelaide. Est-ce que vous êtes malade?"

"Hélas! oui, mon père. J'ai peur que j'étudie trop. Go on, Elizabeth, I'm afraid the bell will ring."

Thus adjured, Elizabeth continued: "There are many young people whose predominant passion is a certain ill-humour, fretfulness, peevishness, or irritability, which pervades their words, manners, and even looks. It is usually brought into action by such mere trifles that there is no chance of peace for those who live in the house with them. Even their best friends are not always secure from their ill-tempered sallies, their quarrelsome moods. Pettish and perverse, they throw a gloom over the gayest hour, and the most innocent amusement. As this luckless disposition is peculiarly that of women, young girls cannot be too earnestly recommended to combat the tendency in youth, lest they become, when older, the torment of that society they are intended to bless and ornament."

Another pause,—a short one this time. Elizabeth's eyes met mine with an unspoken question, and I nodded acquiescence. "Tony!" we breathed simultaneously.

It was true. Tony's engaging qualities were marred by a most prickly temper. We knew her value well. She played all games so admirably that the certainty of defeat modified our pleasure in playing with her. She was fleet of foot, ready of wit, and had more fun in her little brown head than all the rest of us could muster. She would plunge us into abysses of mischief with one hand, and extricate us miraculously with the other. She was startlingly truthful, and lived nobly up to our wayward but scrupulous standard of schoolgirl honour, to the curious code of ethics by which we regulated our lives. She might have been Elizabeth's vice-regent; she might even have disputed the authority of our constitutional sovereign, and have led us Heaven knows whither, had it not been for her pestilential quarrelsomeness. How often had she and I started out at the recreation hour in closest amity, and had returned, silent and glowering, with the wide gravel walk between us. If she were in a fractious mood, no saint from Paradise could have kept the peace. Therefore, when Elizabeth looked at me, we said "Tony!" and then stopped short. She was our friend, one of the band, and though we granted her derelictions, we would not discuss them. We could be ribald enough at Adelaide Harrison's expense, but not at Tony's.

"Why don't you lend her this book?" said Elizabeth kindly.

I shook my head. I knew why very well. And I rather think Elizabeth did, too.

By this time it looked as if we were going to fit the whole school with predominant passions, and not find any for ourselves; but the next line

Elizabeth read struck a chill into my soul, and, as she went on, every word seemed like a barbed arrow aimed unswervingly at me.

"A propensity to extravagant partialities is a fault which frequently predominates in some warm, impetuous characters. These persons are distinguished by a precipitate selection of favourites in every society; by an overflow of marked attentions to the objects of their predilection, whose interests they espouse, whose very faults they attempt to justify, whose opinions they support, whether right or wrong, and whose cause they defend, often at the expense of good sense, charity, moderation, and even common justice. Woe to him who ventures to dissent from them. The friendship or affection of such characters does not deserve to be valued, for it results, not from discernment of merit, but from blind prejudice. Besides, they annoy those whom they think proper to rank among their favourites by expecting to engross their whole attention, and by resenting every mark of kindness they may think proper to show to others. However, as their affections are in general as short-lived as they are ardent, no one person is likely to be long tormented with the title of their friend."

I was conscious of two flaming cheeks as we walked for a moment in silence, and I glanced at Elizabeth out of the tail of my eye to see if she were summing up my case. It wasn't true, it couldn't be true, that extravagant partialities (when they were *my* partialities) were short-lived. I was preparing to combat this part of the accusation when Elizabeth's cool voice dispelled my groundless fears.

"I think that's silly," she said. "Nobody is like that."

The suddenness of my relief made me laugh outright, and then,—Oh, baseness of the human heart!—I sought to strengthen my own position by denouncing some one else. "Not Annie Churchill?" I asked.

Elizabeth considered. "No, not even Annie Churchill. What makes you think of her?"

It was an awkward question. How could I say that two nights before the retreat, Annie had slipped into my alcove,—a reprehensible habit she had,—and, with an air of mystery, had informed me she was "trying to do something,"—she didn't like to tell me what, because she thought that maybe I was trying to do it, too. Upon my intimating that I was trying to go to bed, and nothing else that I knew of, she had said quite solemnly: "I am trying to gain Elizabeth's affections." As it was impossible for me to adduce this piece of evidence (even an unsought confidence we held sacred), I observed somewhat lamely: "Oh, she does seem to get suddenly fond of people."

"Who's she fond of?" asked the unsuspecting—and ungrammatical—Elizabeth.

"Oh, do go on!" I urged, and, even as I said it, the Benediction bell rang. A score of girls, serious, black-veiled young penitents, appeared, as if by magic, hastening to the chapel. We joined them silently, and filed into rank. Already my conscience was pricking. Had our "serious" conversation been either charitable or edifying? Was it for this that Madame Rayburn had sent us out to walk under the mulberry trees?

It pricked harder still—this sore little conscience—the next day, when Lilly came to me, looking downcast and miserable. "Madame Duncan said I might speak to you," she whispered, "because it was about something important. It *is* important, very. Father Santarius is sure to tell us we must put those straws back, and I've broken one of mine."

Straws! I stared at her aghast. Where were my straws? I didn't know. I hadn't the faintest idea. I had lost them both, as I lost everything else, except the empty head so firmly, yet so uselessly fixed upon my shoulders. It was really wonderful that a little girl who had only three places in the world in which to put anything—a desk, a washstand drawer, and a japanned dressing-case (our clothes were all kept for us with exquisite neatness in the vestry)—should not have known where her few possessions were; but I could have lost them all in any of these receptacles, and never have found one of them again. When a mad scramble through my desk had furnished incontestable proof that no straws were there, and Lilly had departed, somewhat comforted by my more desperate case, I sat gloomily facing the complicated problem before me. I must confess my sin, I would be called upon to make restitution, and I had nothing to restore. The more I thought about it, the more hopeless I grew, and the more confused became my sense of proportion. If I had stolen the Bambino himself,—as a peasant woman, it is said, once stole the Baby of Ara-Cœli,—I could not have felt guiltier.

"Agnes," said Madame Rayburn's voice, "you had better go to the chapel now, and prepare for confession."

She was looking down on me, and, as I rose to my feet, a light broke in upon my darkness. I knew where to turn for help.

"If you've taken a thing, and you haven't got it any more to give it back, what can you do?" I asked.

The suddenness with which my query was launched (I always hated roundabout approaches) startled even this seasoned nun. "If you've taken a thing," she echoed. "Do you mean stolen?"

"Yes," I answered stolidly.

She looked astonished for a moment, and then the shadow of a smile passed over her face. "Is it something you have eaten?" she asked, "and that is why you cannot give it back?"

I laughed a little miserable laugh. It was natural that this solution of the problem should present itself to Madame Rayburn's mind, albeit we were not in the fruit season. But then, it had once happened that a collation had been set for the Archbishop and some accompanying priests in the conference room, and that Elizabeth, Lilly, and I, spying through a half-open door the tempting array of sandwiches and cake, had descended like Harpies upon the feast. This discreditable incident lingered, it was plain, in Madame Rayburn's memory, and prompted her question.

"No, it wasn't anything to eat," I said; and then, recognizing the clemency of her mood (she was not always clement), I revealed the sacrilegious nature of my spoliation. "And I've lost them, and can't put them back," I wound up sorrowfully.

Madame Rayburn looked grave. Whether it was because she was shocked, or because she was amused and wanted to conceal her amusement, I cannot say. "Did you do this by yourself?" she said; and then, seeing my face, added hastily: "No, I won't ask you that question. It isn't fair, and besides, I know you won't answer. But if there are any more straws in anybody's possession, I want you to bring them to me to-night. That's all. Now go to confession. Say you've told, and that it's all right."

I was dismissed. With a light heart I sped to the chapel. To see one's way clear through the intricacies of life; to be sure of one's next step, and of a few steps to follow,—at eleven, or at threescore and ten, this is beatitude.

It was Saturday morning when we emerged from retreat, a clear, warm Saturday in June. Mass was over, and we filed down in measureless content to the refectory. Because of our four days' silence, we were permitted to speak our blessed mother tongue at breakfast time. Therefore, instead of the dejected murmur which was the liveliest expression of our Gallic eloquence, there rose upon the startled air a clamorous uproar, a high, shrill, joyous torrent of sound. A hundred girls were talking fast and furiously to make up for lost time. We had hot rolls for breakfast, too, a luxury reserved for such special occasions; and we were all going to the woods in the afternoon, both First and Second Cours,—going for two long, lovely hours, which would give us time to reach the farthest limits of our territory. Elizabeth came and squeezed herself on the bench beside me, to propose a private search for the white violets that grew in the marshy ground beyond the lake, and that bloomed long after the wood violets had gone. Tony shouted across two intervening benches that she didn't see why we could not secure the boat, and have a row,—as if the Second Cours girls were at all likely to get possession of the boat when the First Cours girls were around. "We can, if we try," persisted Tony, in whom four days of peaceful meditation had bred the liveliest inclination for a brawl. As for me, I ate my roll, and looked out of the window at the charming vista stretching down to the woods; and my spirits mounted higher and higher with the rising tide of joy, with the glad return to the life of every day. Heaven, an assured hereafter, had receded comfortably into the dim future. Hell was banished from our apprehensions. But, oh, how beautiful was the world!

Un Congé sans Cloche

WE had only two or three of them in the year, and their slow approach stirred us to frenzy. In the dark ages, when I went to school, no one had yet discovered that play is more instructive than work, no one was piling up statistics to prove the educational value of idleness. In the absence of nature studies and athletics, we were not encouraged to spend our lives out of doors. In the absence of nerve specialists, we were not tenderly restrained from studying our lessons too hard. It is wonderful how little apprehension on this score was felt by either mothers or teachers. We had two months' summer holiday,—July and August,—and a week at Christmas time. The rest of the year we spent at school. I have known parents so inhuman as to regret those unenlightened days.

But can the glorified little children whose lives seem now to be one vast and happy playtime, can the privileged schoolgirls who are permitted to come to town for a matinée,—which sounds to me as fairy-like as Cinderella's ball,—ever know the real value of a holiday? As well expect an infant millionaire to know the real value of a quarter. We to whom the routine of life was as inevitable as the progress of the seasons, we to whom Saturdays were as Mondays, and who grappled with Church history and Christian doctrine on pleasant Sunday mornings, *we* knew the mad tumultuous joy that thrilled through hours of freedom. The very name which from time immemorial had been given to our convent holidays illustrated the fulness of their beatitude. When one lives under the dominion of bells, every hour rung in and out with relentless precision, *sans cloche* means glorious saturnalia. Once a nervous young nun, anxious at the wild scattering of her flock, ventured, on a *congé*, to ring them back to bounds; whereupon her bell was promptly, though not unkindly, taken away from her by two of the older girls. And when the case was brought to court, the Mistress General upheld their action. A law was a law, as binding upon its officers as upon the smallest subject in the realm.

The occasions for a *congé sans cloche* were as august as they were rare. "Mother's Feast," by which we meant the saint's day of the Superioress, could always be reckoned upon. The feast of St. Joseph was also kept in this auspicious fashion,—which gave us a great "devotion" to so kind a mediator. Once or twice in the year the Archbishop came to the convent, and in return for our addresses, our curtsies, our baskets of flowers, and songs of welcome, always bravely insisted that we should have a holiday. "Be sure and tell me, if you don't get it," he used to say, which sounded charmingly confidential, though we well knew that we should never have an opportunity to tell him anything of the kind, and that we should never dare to do it, if we had.

In the year of grace which I now chronicle, the Archbishop was going to Rome, and had promised to say good-by to us before he sailed. Those were troubled times for Rome. Even we knew that something was wrong, though our information did not reach far beyond this point. Like the little girl who couldn't tell where Glasgow was, because she had not finished studying Asia Minor, we were still wandering belated in the third Crusade,—a far cry from united Italy. When Elizabeth, who had read the address, said she wondered why the Pope was called "God's great martyr saint," we could offer her very little enlightenment. I understand that children now interest themselves in current events, and ask intelligent questions about things they read in the newspapers. For us, the Wars of the Roses were as yesterday, and the Crusades were still matters for deep concern. Berengaria of Navarre had been the "leading lady" of our day's lesson, and I had written in my "Compendium of History"—majestic phrase—this interesting and comprehensive statement: "Berengaria led a blameless life, and, after her husband's death, retired to a monastery, where she passed the remainder of her days."

It was the middle of May when the Archbishop came, and, as the weather was warm, we wore our white frocks for the occasion. Very immaculate we looked, ranged in a deep, shining semicircle, a blue ribbon around every neck, and gloves on every folded hand. It would have been considered the height of impropriety to receive, ungloved, a distinguished visitor. As the prelate entered, accompanied by the Superioress and the Mistress General, we swept him a deep curtsy,—oh, the hours of bitter practice it took to limber my stiff little knees for those curtsies!—and then broke at once into our chorus of welcome:—

"With happy hearts we now repair

All in this joyous scene to share."

There were five verses. When we had finished, we curtsied again and sat down, while Mary Rawdon and Eleanor Hale played a nervous duet upon the piano.

The Archbishop looked at us benignantly. It was said of him that he dearly loved children, but that he was apt to be bored by adults. He had not what are called "social gifts," and seldom went beyond the common civilities of intercourse. But he would play jackstraws all evening with half a dozen children, and apparently find himself much refreshed by the entertainment. His eyes wandered during the duet to the ends of the semicircle, where sat the very little girls, as rigidly still as cataleptics. Wriggling was not then deemed the prescriptive right of childhood. An acute observer might perhaps have thought that the Archbishop, seated majestically on his dais, and flanked by Reverend Mother and Madame Bouron, glanced wistfully at these motionless little figures. We were, in truth, as remote from him as if we had been on another continent. Easy familiarity with our superiors was a thing undreamed of in our philosophy. The standards of good behaviour raised an impassable barrier between us.

Frances Fenton made the address. It was an honour once accorded to Elizabeth, but usually reserved as a reward for superhuman virtue. Not on *that* score had Elizabeth ever enjoyed it. Frances was first blue ribbon, first medallion, and head of the Children of Mary. There was nothing left for her but beatification. She stepped slowly, and with what was called a "modest grace," into the middle of the room, curtsied, and began:—

"Your children's simple hearts would speak,

But cannot find the words they seek.

These tones no music's spell can lend;

And eloquence would vainly come

To greet our Father, Guide, and Friend.

Let hearts now speak, and lips be dumb!"

"Then why isn't she dumb?" whispered Tony aggressively, but without changing a muscle of her attentive face.

I pretended not to hear her. I had little enough discretion, Heaven knows, but even I felt the ripe unwisdom of whispering at such a time. It was Mary Rawdon's absence, at the piano, I may observe, that placed me in this perilous proximity.

"Our reverence fond and hopeful prayer

Will deck with light one empty place,

And fill with love one vacant chair."

"What chair?" asked Tony, and again I pretended not to hear.

"For e'en regret can wear a softened grace,

And smiling hope in whispers low

Will oft this cherished thought bestow:

Within the Eternal City's sacred wall,

He who has blest us in our Convent hall

Can now to us earth's holiest blessing bring

From God's great martyr saint, Rome's pontiff king."

At this point, Tony, maddened by my unresponsiveness, shot out a dexterous little leg (I don't see how she dared to do it, when our skirts were so short), and, with lightning speed, kicked me viciously on the shins. The anguish was acute, but my sense of self-preservation saved me from so much as a grimace. Madame Bouron's lynx-like gaze was travelling down our ranks, and, as it rested on me for an instant, I felt that she must see the smart. Tony's expression was one of rapt and reverent interest. By the time I had mastered my emotions, and collected my thoughts, the address was over, and the Archbishop was saying a few words about his coming voyage, and about the Holy Father, for whom he bade us pray. Then, with commendable promptness, he broached the important subject of the *congé*. There was the usual smiling demur on Reverend Mother's part. The children had so many holidays ("I like that!" snorted Tony), so many interruptions to their work. It was so hard to bring them back again to quiet and orderly ways. If she granted this indulgence, we must promise to study with double diligence for the approaching examinations. Finally she yielded, as became a dutiful daughter of the Church; the first of June, ten days off, was fixed as the date; and we gave a hearty round of applause, in token of our gratitude and relief. After this, we rather expected our august visitor to go away; but his eyes had strayed again to the motionless little girls at the horns of the semicircle; and, as if they afforded him an inspiration, he said something in low, rather urgent tones to Reverend Mother,—something to which she listened graciously.

"They will be only too proud and happy," we heard her murmur; and then she raised her voice.

"Children," she said impressively, "his Grace is good enough to ask that you should escort him to the woods this afternoon. Put on your hats and go."

This *was* an innovation! Put on our hats at four o'clock—the hour for French class—and walk to the woods with the Archbishop. It was delightful, of course, but a trifle awesome. If, in his ignorance, he fancied we should gambol around him like silly lambs, he was soon to discover his mistake. Our line of march more closely resembled that of a well-drilled army. Madame Bouron walked on his right hand, and Madame Duncan on his left. The ribbons, the graduates, and a few sedate girls from the first class closed into a decorous group, half of them walking backwards,—a convent custom in which we were wonderfully expert. The flanks of the army were composed of younger and less distinguished girls, while the small fry hovered on its borders, out of sight and hearing. We moved slowly, without scattering, and without obvious exhilaration. I was occupied in freeing my mind in many bitter words to Tony, who defended her conduct on the score of my "setting up for sainthood,"—an accusation the novelty of which ought to have made it agreeable.

When we reached the lake, a tiny sheet of water with a Lilliputian island, we came to a halt. The Archbishop had evidently expressed some desire, or at least some readiness, to trust himself upon the waves. The boat was unmoored, and Frances Fenton and Ella Holrook rowed him carefully around the island, while the rest of us were drawn up on shore to witness the performance. We made, no doubt, a very nice picture in our white frocks and blue neck ribbons; but we were spectators merely, still far remote from any sense of companionship. When the boat was close to shore, the Archbishop refused to land. He sat in the stern, looking at us with a curious smile. He was strikingly handsome,—a long, lean, noble-looking old man,—and he had a voice of wonderful sweetness and power. It was said that, even at sixty-five, he sang the Mass more beautifully than any priest in his diocese. Therefore it was a little alarming when he suddenly asked:—

"My children, do you know any pretty songs?"

"Oh, yes, your Grace," answered Madame Bouron.

"Then sing me something now," said the Archbishop, still with that inscrutable smile.

There was a moment's hesitation, a moment's embarrassment, and then, acting under instruction, we sang (or, at least, some of us did; there was no music in my soul) the "Canadian Boat-Song," and "Star of the Sea,"—appropriate, both of them, to the watery expanse before us.

"*Ave Maria*, we lift our eyes to thee;

Ora pro nobis; 'tis night far o'er the sea."

The Archbishop listened attentively, and with an evident pleasure that must have been wholly disassociated from any musical sense. Then his smile deepened. "Would you like me to sing for you?" he said.

"Oh, yes, if you please," we shrilled; and Madame Bouron gave us a warning glance. "Be very still, children," she admonished. "His Grace is going to sing."

His Grace settled himself comfortably in the boat. His amused glance travelled over our expectant faces, and sought as usual the little girls, now close to the water's edge. Then he cleared his throat, and, as I am a Christian gentlewoman, and a veracious chronicler, *this* is the song he sang:—

"In King Arthur's reign, a merry reign,

Three children were sent from their homes,

Were sent from their homes, were sent from their homes,

And they never went back again.

"The first, he was a miller,

The second, he was a weaver,

The third, he was a little tailor boy,

Three big rogues together."

"Can't you join in the chorus, children?" interrupted the Archbishop. "Come! the last two lines of every verse."

"The third, he was a little tailor boy,

Three big rogues together."

Our voices rose in a quavering accompaniment to his mellifluous notes. We were petrified; but, even in a state of petrification, we did as we were bidden.

"The miller, he stole corn,

The weaver, he stole yarn,

And the little tailor boy, he stole broadcloth,

To keep these three rogues warm."

"Chorus!" commanded the Archbishop; and this time our voices were louder and more assured.

"And the little tailor boy, he stole broadcloth,

To keep these three rogues warm."

"The miller was drowned in his dam,

The weaver was hung by his yarn,

But the Devil ran away with the little tailor boy,

With the broadcloth under his arm."

There was a joyous shout from our ranks. We understood it all now. The Archbishop was misbehaving himself, was flaunting his misbehaviour in Madame Bouron's face. We knew very well what would be said to us, if we sang a song like that, without the Archiepiscopal sanction, and there was a delicious sense of impunity in our hearts, as we vociferated the unhallowed lines:—

"But the Devil ran away with the little tailor boy,

With the broadcloth under his arm."

Then the Archbishop stepped out of the boat, and there was a timid scramble to his side. The barriers were down. He had knocked at our hearts in the Devil's name, and we had flung them wide. The return to the convent was like a rout;—little girls wedging their way in among big girls, the Second Cours contesting every step of the path with the First Cours, the most insignificant children lifted suddenly to prominence and distinction. I was too shy to do more than move restlessly on the outskirts of the crowd; but I saw Tony conversing affably with the Archbishop (and looking as gentle as she was intelligent), and Viola Milton kissing his ring with the assurance of an infant Aloysius. When he bade us good-by, we shouted and waved our handkerchiefs until he was out of sight. He turned at the end of the avenue, and waved his in a last friendly salutation. That was very long ago. I trust that in Paradise the Holy Innocents are now bearing him company, for I truly believe his soul would weary of the society of grown-up saints.

And our *congé* was only ten days off. This thought was left to gild our waking hours. We—Elizabeth, Marie, Tony, Lilly, Emily, and I—resolved ourselves immediately into a committee of ways and means, and voted all the money in the treasury for supplies. It was not much, but, if well laid out, it would purchase sweets enough to insure a midnight pang. The privilege of buying so much as a stick of candy was one rigidly reserved for holidays. "Mary" did our shopping for us. Mary was a hybrid, a sort of uncloistered nun. Her out-of-date bonnet, worn instead of a lay sister's close white cap, proclaimed her as one free to come and go; and her mission in life was to transact outside business, to buy whatever was necessary or permitted. The lay sisters did the work of the convent; Mary ministered to its needs. We wrote down for her a list of delicacies.

One dozen oranges.

One box of figs.

One pound of caramels,—which were dear.

Two pounds of walnut taffy.

Three pounds of cinnamon bun.

A fair allowance, I surmise, for six well-fed little girls.

"I tell you what I'll do," said Marie, in an excess of generosity. "I'll save up my wine, if you'll lend me bottles to put it in."

We felt this to be noble. For some mysterious reason (she was never known to be ill), Marie was sent every morning at eleven o'clock to the infirmary; and at that unconvivial hour drank a solitary glass of wine. It was port, I believe, or Burgundy,—I am not sure which, and I pray Heaven I may never taste its like again. Now, provided with half a dozen empty bottles, which had erstwhile held tooth-wash and cologne, she undertook to elude the infirmarian's eye, and to decant her wine into these receptacles, instead of putting it where it was due. How she managed this we never knew (it would have seemed difficult to a prestidigitator), but Marie was a child of resources, second only to Tony in every baleful art.

Clever though we deemed her, however, clever though we sometimes deemed ourselves, there was one in the school, younger, yet far more acute than any of us. Thursday was visitors' day, and Lilly's brother came to see her. After he had gone, Lilly joined us in the avenue, looking perturbed and mysterious.

"I want to tell you something," she said lamely. "Viola has got some cigarettes. Jack gave them to her."

Cigarettes! Dynamite could not have sounded more overwhelming. Cigarettes, and in Viola Milton's keeping! Never had a whiff of tobacco defiled the convent air. Never had the thought of such unbridled license entered into any heart. And Viola was ten years old.

"I know what that means," said Tony sharply. "She wants to come with us on the *congé*."

Lilly nodded. It was plain that Viola, having possessed herself of a heavy bribe, had persuaded her older sister to open negotiations.

"Well, we won't have her," cried Tony vehemently. "Not if she has all the cigarettes in Christendom. Why on earth, Lilly, didn't you ask your brother for them yourself?"

"I never thought of such a thing," pleaded Lilly. "I never even heard her do it."

"Well, we won't have Viola, and you may go and tell her so," repeated Tony with mounting wrath. "Go and tell her so right off. We won't have a child of ten tagging round with us all day."

"Agnes is only eleven," said Lilly.

"How many cigarettes has she got?" It was Elizabeth who asked this pertinent question.

"I don't know. Jack gave her all he had."

"It doesn't make any difference how many she has. I won't have her," flamed Tony.

At this assertive "I," Elizabeth lifted her head. Her light blue eyes met Tony's sparkling brown ones. It was not the first time the two children had measured their forces. "We'll see, anyhow, what Viola's got," said Elizabeth calmly.

Lilly, being despatched to make inquiries, returned in two minutes with her little sister by her side. Viola was a bony child, all eyes and teeth, as ugly as Lilly was beautiful. Her sombre glance was riveted wistfully upon Elizabeth's face. She was too wise to weaken her cause with words, but held out eleven little white objects, at which we looked enviously.

"Seven from eleven leaves four," murmured Emily.

"I don't want any," said Viola, who was bidding high. She would have bartered her immortal soul to gain her point.

"And I don't want more than one," said Lilly. "That will leave two apiece for the rest of you."

"Well?" asked Elizabeth, looking round the circle.

"Oh, do let's have them!" I urged, dazzled by a sudden vision of debauchery. "They'll be just the thing to go with the wine."

They were *just* the thing. We found this out later on.

"Oh, yes, let's have them," said Marie, who felt the responsibilities of a hostess.

"Let's," said Emily, our silent member.

"I won't!" asseverated Tony, battling heroically for a lost cause. "I won't have anything to do with the treat, if you let Viola in."

"Then don't!" retorted Elizabeth, now sure of victory, and scornful of further dispute.

Tony turned her back upon her venal friends, and marched off to another group of girls. There was no great novelty about this proceeding, but the imminence of the *congé* lent it an unwonted seriousness.

"Don't you suppose she'll play *cache cache* with us?" asked Marie somewhat ruefully, and well aware of what we should lose if she did not.

"Of course she will," said Elizabeth, "because she can't play without us."

And Elizabeth was right. Before the first of June, Tony had "come round;" being persuaded to this condescension by Lilly the peacemaker. Every cluster of friends should look to it that there is one absolutely sweet-tempered person in the group. But one is enough.

The first glorious thing about a *congé* was that we got up at seven instead of at quarter-past six, and the next was that we began to talk before we were out of our beds. Breakfast was so hilarious that only the fear of wasting our precious hours ever dragged us from the refectory, and up into the schoolroom, to prepare for the special feature of the day, *cache cache*. We never played *cache cache* except upon a holiday, which was why it seemed such a thrilling and wonderful game. No indulgence was likely to lose its value for us through unwarranted repetition. Two captains were chosen by acclamation, and they in turn elected their girls, picking them out alternately, one by one, until the whole Second Cours was divided into two bands of about twenty each. One band remained shut up in a music room (which was goal) for half an hour, while the other betook itself to the most secret and inaccessible spot that could be thought of as a hiding place. The captain might stay with her band, and direct its action, or she might be hidden separately; but no one except the captain was permitted to stray from the ranks for purposes of reconnoitring. The same rule held good for the searching party. The captain alone might play the scout. The rest were obliged to hold together. The capture of the hidden captain counted as half the game. The capture of the hidden band, before it could reach its goal, counted as the other half of the game. Thus the hiders were forced either to dispense with the invaluable services of their leader, or to risk the loss of the whole game, if she were surprised in their company. So much, indeed, depended upon the leader's tactics, and so keen was our thirst for victory, that the girl who saved the day for herself and for her comrades was held in higher esteem than the girl who came out ahead in the periodical blistering of examinations. College valuations are, perhaps, not so absolutely modern as they seem.

Given an area of over a hundred acres, with woods and orchards, with a deep ravine choked with tangled underbrush for concealment, and with wide lawns for an open run,—and *cache cache* becomes, or at least it became for us, a glorious and satisfying sport. To crouch breathless in the "poisonous valley" (there was a touch of poetry in all our nomenclature), to skirt cautiously the marshy ground of La Salette (named after the miraculous spring of Dauphiné), to crawl on one's stomach behind half a mile of inadequate hedge, to make a wild dash for goal within full view of the pursuing party,—these things supplied all the trepidation and fatigue, all the opportunities for generalship, and all the openings for dispute, that reasonable children could demand. We hardly needed the additional excitement provided by Eloise Didier's slipping into the marsh, and being fished out, a compact cake of mud; or by Tony's impiously hiding in the organ loft of the chapel, and being caught red-handed by Madame Duncan,—a nun whom, thank Heaven! it was possible, though difficult, to cajole.

We played all morning and all afternoon, played until our strength and our spirits were alike exhausted; and then, when the shadows began to lengthen, and our vivacity to wane, we made ready for the mad carousal which was to close our day. A basement music room, as remote as possible from any chance of inspection, was chosen as the scene of revelry. It was not a cheerful spot; but it appeared reasonably safe. Hither we transported our feast, which, spread out upon a piano, presented a formidable appearance, and restored us to gayety and good humour. The advantage of childhood over riper years is its blessed slowness to recognize a failure. If a thing starts out to be a treat, why, it *is* a treat, and that's the end of it. The cinnamon bun was certainly stale (Mary had, it was plain, consulted her own convenience as to the day of its purchase), but Heaven forbid that we should balk at staleness. Oranges and caramels, figs and walnut taffy present, to the thinking mind, an inharmonious combination; but that was a point on which we were to be subsequently enlightened. As for Marie's wine, it can be readily imagined what *it* was like, after lying around for a warm May week in imperfectly corked tooth-wash bottles. I can only say that no medicine it had been my lot to taste was ever half so nasty; yet those were days when all drugs were of uncompromising bitterness. An effete civilization had not then devised gelatine capsules to defraud the palate of its pain.

We ate everything, cake, fruit, and candy; we drank the wine (heroic young souls!), and, trembling with excitement, we lit the cigarettes,— a more difficult matter than we had imagined. I had not waited until this point to dree my weird. Excessive fatigue is but an indifferent preparation for unwonted indulgence; and I was a sickly child, to whom only the simplicity and regularity of school life lent a semblance of health. Ominous sensations were warning me of my deadly peril; but I held straight on. Suddenly Marie, who had been smoking with silent fortitude, said sweetly:

"It's a shame Viola shouldn't have one of her own cigarettes. I'll give her my second."

"She can have one of mine, too," said Emily.

"Thank you," returned Viola hastily. "I don't want any. I gave them to you."

"Oh, do try one!" urged Marie.

"Yes, do!" said Tony sardonically. "Do try one, Viola. They are anxious enough to get rid of them."

She flung this taunt at the crowd, but her eye met mine with a challenge I would not evade. "I want my second one," I said.

Valour met valour. "So do I," smiled Tony.

From this point, my recollections are vague. We talked about Madame Davide, and whether she really did not understand English, or only pretended not to,—a point which had never been satisfactorily settled. We talked about Madame Bouron, and her methods (which we deemed unworthy) of finding out all she knew. I added little to the sprightliness of the conversation, and after a while I slipped away. On the stairs a kindly fate threw me into the arms of Sister O'Neil, who had charge of the vestry, and who was carrying piles of clean linen to the dormitories. She was a friendly soul (nearly all the lay sisters were good to us), and she took possession of me then and there. When I was safe in bed,—collapsed but comforted,—she sprinkled me with holy water, and tucked the light covers carefully around me. "Lie quiet now," she said. "I'll go tell Madame Rayburn where you are, and that there was no time to ask leave of anybody."

I did lie very quiet, and, after a while, fell into a doze, from which the sound of footsteps woke me. Some one was standing at the foot of my bed. It was Tony. She looked a trifle more sallow than usual, but was grinning cheerfully. "I'm better now," she said.

The delicate emphasis on the *now* was like a condensed epic. "So am I," I murmured confidentially.

Tony disappeared, and in a few minutes was back again, comfortably attired in a dressing gown and slippers. She perched herself on the foot of my bed. "Hasn't it been a perfect *congé*?" she sighed happily. (Oh, blessed memory of youth!) "If you'd seen Madame Duncan, though, when I came stealing out of the chapel,—without a veil, too. 'What does this mean, Tony?' she said. 'It isn't possible that'"—

There was an abrupt pause. "Well?" I asked expectantly, though I had heard it all several times already; but Tony's eyes were fixed on the little pile of clean linen lying on my chair.

"Oh! I say," she cried, and there was a joyous ring in her voice. "Here's our chance. Let's change all the girls' washes."

I gazed at her with heartfelt admiration. To have passed recently through so severe a crisis,—a crisis which had reduced me to nothingness; and yet to be able instantly to think of such a charming thing to do. Not for the first time, I felt proud of Tony's friendship. Her resourcefulness compelled my homage. Had we been living in one of Mr. James's novels, I should have called her "great" and "wonderful."

"Get up and help," said Tony.

I stumbled out of bed, and into my slippers. My head felt curiously light when I lifted it from my pillow, and I had to catch hold of my curtain rod for support. The dormitory floor heaved up and down. Tony was already at work, carrying the linen from one side of the room to the other, and I staggered weakly after her. There were thirty beds, so it took us some time to accomplish our mission; but "The labour we delight in physics pain;" and it was with a happy heart, and a sense of exalted satisfaction, that I saw the last pile safe in the wrong alcove, and crawled back between my sheets.—"Something attempted, something done, to earn a night's repose." Tony sat on my bed, and we talked confidentially until we heard the girls coming upstairs. Then she fled, and I awaited developments.

They entered more noisily than was their wont. The law ruled that a *congé* came to an end with night prayers, after which no word might be spoken; but it was hard to control children who had been demoralized by a long day of liberty. Moreover, the "Seven Dolours" dormitory was ever the most turbulent of the three; its inmates lacking the docility of the very little girls, and the equanimity of the big ones. They were all at what is called the troublesome age. There was a note of anxiety in Madame Chapelle's voice, as she hushed down some incipient commotion.

"I must have perfect silence in the dormitory," she said. "You have talked all day; now you must go quietly to bed. Do you hear me, children? Silence!"

There was a lull, and then—I knew it must soon come—a voice from the far end of the room. "I have thirty-seven's clothes" (everything was marked with our school numbers), "instead of mine."

"Mary Aylmer, be quiet!" commanded Madame Chapelle.

"But, Madame, I tell you truly, I have thirty-seven's clothes. Who is thirty-seven?"

"I am," cried another voice,—Eloise Didier's. "But I haven't got your clothes, Mary Aylmer. I've got Alice Campbell's. Here, Alice,—twenty-two,—come take your things."

"Who is thirty-three? Ruffled night-gown with two buttons off. Oh, shame!" sang out Marie jubilantly.

"Children, will you be silent!" said Madame Chapelle, angry and bewildered. "What do you mean by such behaviour?"

"Forty-two's stockings want darning," said a reproachful voice. It was very probable, for I was forty-two.

"So do thirty-eight's."

"Adelaide H. McC. Harrison," Elizabeth read slowly, and with painstaking precision. "Haven't you any more initials, Adelaide, you could have put on your underclothes?"

"Look again, Elizabeth. Surely there's a coronet somewhere?" interposed Eloise Didier sardonically. Adelaide was not popular in our community.

"Three coronets, a sceptre, and a globe," said Elizabeth.

"Children," began Madame Chapelle; but her voice was lost in the scurrying of feet, as girl after girl darted across the polished floor to claim her possessions, or to rid herself of some one else's. They were, I well knew, devoutly grateful for this benign confusion, and were making the most of it. Fate did not often throw such chances in their way. For a moment I felt that noble joy which in this world is granted only to successful effort, to the accomplishment of some well-planned, well-executed design. Then silence fell suddenly upon the room, and I knew, though I could not see, that every girl was back in her own alcove.

"May I ask the meaning of this disorder!" said Madame Rayburn coldly.

She was *surveillante*, and was making the round of the dormitories, to see that everything was quiet after the day's excitement. Madame Chapelle began a nervous explanation. There was some mistake about the laundry. None of the children had their own clothes. They were trying—rather noisily, she admitted—to exchange them. Was it possible that Sister O'Neil—

"Sister O'Neil!" interrupted Madame Rayburn impatiently. "Sister O'Neil had nothing to do with it. Answer me quietly, children. Did you all find you had some one else's clothes?"

There was a murmur of assent,—a polite, subdued, apologetic sort of murmur; but, none the less, of universal assent. At that instant I remembered Sister O'Neil's parting words to me, and, with the instinctive impulse of the ostrich, slid deeper in my little bed. A quick step crossed the dormitory. A firm hand drew my curtain. "Agnes!" said Madame Rayburn, in a terrible voice.

Ah, well! Anyway, the *congé* was over.

Marriage Vows

We had decided upon the married estate, titles, and foreign travel. I do not mean that we cherished such ambitions for the future,—what was the future to us?—but that in the world of illusions, which was our world, we were about to assume these new and dazzling conditions. Childish even for our years, though our years were very few, and preserved mercifully from that familiar and deadening intercourse with adults, which might have resulted in our being sensible and well informed, we cultivated our imaginations instead of our minds. The very bareness of our surroundings, the absence of all appliances for play, flung us back unreservedly upon the illimitable resources of invention. It was in the long winter months, when nature was unkind, when the last chestnut had been gathered, and the last red leaf pressed carefully in an atlas, that we awoke to the recognition of our needs, and slipped across the border-land of fancy. It was then that certain wise and experienced nuns watched us closely, knowing that our pent-up energies might at any moment break down the barriers of discipline; but knowing also that it was not possible for a grown-up person, however well disposed, to enter our guarded realm. We were always under observation, but the secret city wherein we dwelt was trodden by no other foot than ours.

It had rained for a week. We had exhausted the resources of literature and the drama. A new book in the convent library, a book with a most promising title, "The Witch of Melton Hill," had turned out to be a dismal failure. Elizabeth observed sardonically that if it had been named, as it should have been, "The Guardian Angel of Hallam House," we should at least have let it alone. An unreasoning relative had sent me as a belated Christmas gift, "Agnes Hilton; or Pride Corrected,"—making the feeble excuse that I bore the heroine's name. To a logical mind this would have seemed no ground either for giving me the story, or for blaming me because it proved unreadable. But Tony, to whom I lent it, reproached me with exceeding bitterness for having the kind of a name—a goody-goody name she called it—which was always borne by pious and virtuous heroines. She said she thanked Heaven none of them were ever christened Antoinette; and she seemed to hold me responsible for the ennobling qualities she despised.

As for the drama, we had acted for the second time Elizabeth's masterpiece, "The Youth of Michael Angelo," and there appeared to be no further opening for our talents. We little girls, with the imitative instincts of our age, were always endeavouring to reproduce on a modest scale the artistic triumphs with which the big girls entertained the school. It was hard work, because we had no plays, no costumes, and no manager. We had only Elizabeth, who rose to the urgent needs of the situation, overcoming for our sake the aversion she felt for any form of composition, and substituting for her French exercises the more inspiring labours of the dramatist. Her first attempt was slight, a mere curtain raiser, and dealt with the fortunes of a robber chief, who, after passionate pursuit of a beautiful and beloved maiden, finds out that she is his sister, and hails the news with calm fraternal joy. By a fortunate coincidence, he also discovers that an aged traveller whom he had purposed robbing is his father; so the curtain falls upon a united family, the gentle desperado quoting an admirable sentiment of Cowper's (it was in our reader, accompanied by a picture of a gentleman, a lady, a baby, and a bird-cage):—

"Domestic happiness, thou only bliss

Of Paradise that has survived the fall."

The success of this touching and realistic little play encouraged Elizabeth to more ambitious efforts. She set about dramatizing, with my assistance, a story from "The Boyhood of Great Painters," which told how the youthful Michael Angelo modelled a snow Faun in the gardens of Lorenzo de Medici, and how that magnificent duke, seeing this work of art before it had time to melt, showered praises and promises upon the happy sculptor. It was not a powerful theme, but there was an ancient retainer of the Buonarroti family (Elizabeth wisely reserved this part for herself), who made sarcastic remarks about his employers, and never appeared without a large feather duster, thus fulfilling all the legitimate requirements of modern comedy. What puzzled us most sorely was the Faun, which we supposed to be an innocent young quadruped, and had no possible way of presenting. Therefore, after a great deal of consideration, it was determined that a flower girl should be substituted; this happy idea (so suggestive of Michael Angelo's genius) being inspired by the plaster figures then sadly familiar to lawns and garden walks. In the story, the young artist emphasized the age of the Faun by deftly knocking out two of its front teeth,—a touch of realism beyond our range, as Viola Milton in a night-gown played the statue's part. In our drama, the Duke complained that the flower girl was too grave, whereupon Michael Angelo, with a few happy touches, gave her a smile so broad—Viola's teeth being her most prominent feature—that some foolish little girls in the audience thought a joke was intended, and laughed uproariously.

Marie played Michael Angelo. I was his proud father, who appeared only in the last scene, and said, "Come to my arms, my beloved son!" which he did so impetuously—Marie was nothing if not ardent—that I was greatly embarrassed, and did not know how to hold him. Lorenzo the Magnificent was affably, though somewhat feebly, portrayed by Annie Churchill, who wore a waterproof cloak, flung, like Hamlet's mantle, over her left shoulder, and a beaver hat with a red bow and an ostrich plume, the property of Eloise Didier. It was a significant circumstance that when Marie, rushing to my embrace, knocked over a little table, the sole furniture of the Medicean palace, and indicating by its presence that we were no longer in the snow, Lorenzo hastily picked it up, and straightened the cover; while Elizabeth—who had no business to be in that scene—stood calmly by, twirling her feather duster, and apparently accustomed to being waited on by the flower of the Florentine nobility.

The production of "Michael Angelo" cost us four weeks of hard and happy labour. His name became so familiar to our lips that Tony, whose turn it was to read night and morning prayers, substituted it profanely for that of the blessed Archangel. We always said the Credo and Confiteor in Latin, so that *beato Michaeli Archangelo* became *beato Michael Angelo*, without attracting the attention of any ears save ours. It was one of those daring jests (as close to wickedness as we ever got) which served as passwords in our secret city. The second time we gave the play, we extended a general invitation to the First Cours to come and see it; and a score or so of the less supercilious girls actually availed themselves of the privilege. It is hard for me to make clear what condescension this implied. Feudal lord and feudal vassal were not more widely separated than were the First and Second Cours. Feudal lord and feudal vassal were not more firmly convinced of the justness of their respective positions. No uneasy agitator had ever pricked us into discontent. The existing order of things seemed to us as natural as the planetary system.

Now, casting about for some new form of diversion, Elizabeth proposed one stormy afternoon that we should assume titles, and marry one another; secretly, of course, but with all the pomp and circumstance that imagination could devise. She herself, having first choice, elected England for her dwelling-place, and Emily for her spouse. She took Emily, I am sure, because that silent and impassive child was the only one of the five who didn't particularly covet the honour. Elizabeth, protecting herself instinctively from our affection and admiration, found her natural refuge in this unresponsive bosom. Because Emily would just as soon have married Lilly or me, Elizabeth wisely offered her her hand. She also insisted that Emily, being older, should be husband. Mere surface ambition was alien to her character. The position of *maîtresse femme* satisfied all reasonable requirements.

Names and titles were more difficult of selection. Emily was well disposed toward a dukedom; but Elizabeth preferred that her husband should be an earl, because an earl was "belted," and a duke, we surmised, wasn't.

"A duke is higher than an earl," said the well-informed Emily.

"But he isn't belted," insisted Elizabeth. "It's a 'belted knight' and a 'belted earl' always; never a belted duke. You can wear a belt if you're an earl, Emily."

"I do wear a belt," said the prosaic Emily.

"Then, of course, you've got to be an earl," retorted Elizabeth; reasoning by some process, not perfectly plain to us, but conclusive enough for Emily, who tepidly yielded the point. "Philip Howard, Earl of Arundel"—

"I won't be named Philip," interrupted Emily rebelliously.

"Well, then, Henry Howard, Earl of Arundel and Surrey, and we'll live in Arundel Castle."

"You got that out of 'Constance Sherwood,'" said Marie.

Elizabeth nodded. Lady Fullerton's pretty story had been read aloud in the refectory, and we were rather "up" in English titles as a consequence.

"I'm going to be Prince of Castile," said Tony suddenly.

I leaped from my chair. "You shan't!" I flashed, and then stopped short, bitterly conscious of my impotence. Tony had "spoken first." There was no wresting her honours from her. She knew, she must have known that Castile was the home of my soul, though no one had ever sounded the depth of my devotion. My whole life was lit by Spain's sombre glow. It was the land where my fancy strayed whenever it escaped from thraldom, and to which I paid a secret and passionate homage. The destruction of the Invincible Armada was the permanent sorrow of my childhood. And now Tony had located herself in this paradise of romance. "Castile's proud dames" would be her peers and countrywomen. The Alhambra would be her pleasure-house (geographically I was a trifle indistinct), and Moorish slaves would wait upon her will. I could not even share these blessed privileges, because it was plain to all of us that Tony's one chance of connubial felicity lay in having Lilly for a partner. The divorce courts would have presented a speedy termination to any other alliance.

"Never mind, Agnes," said Marie consolingly. "We don't want Castile. It's a soapy old place. We'll be Duke and Duchess of Tuscany."

I yielded a sorrowful assent. Tuscany awoke no echoes in my bosom. I neither knew nor cared whence Marie had borrowed the suggestion. But the priceless discipline of communal life had taught us all to respect one another's rights, and to obey the inflexible rules of play. Tony had staked her claim to Castile; and I became Beatrice della Rovere, Duchess of Tuscany, without protest, but without elation. Lilly looked genuinely distressed. Her sweet heart was hurt to feel that she was depriving a friend of any happiness, and it is safe to say that she was equally indifferent to the grandeurs of Italy and of Spain. Perhaps Griselda the patient felt no lively concern as to the whereabouts of her husband's estates. She had other and more serious things to ponder.

The marriage ceremony presented difficulties. We must have a priest to officiate; that is, we must have a girl discreet enough to be trusted with our secret, yet stupid enough, or amiable enough, to be put out of the play afterwards. We had no idea of being burdened with clerical society. Annie Churchill was finally chosen for the rôle. Her functions were carefully explained to her, and her scruples—she was dreadfully afraid of doing something wrong—were, by candid argument, overcome. Marie wanted to be married in the "Lily of Judah" chapel, a tiny edifice girt by the winding drive; but Elizabeth firmly upheld the superior claims of St. Joseph.

St. Joseph was, as we well knew, the patron of marriage, its advocate and friend. We depended upon him to find us our future husbands,—in which regard he has shown undue partiality,—and it was in good faith that we now placed ourselves under his protection. Our play inevitably reflected the religious influences by which we were so closely environed. I hear it said that the little sons of ministers preach to imaginary audiences in the nursery,—an idea which conveys a peculiar horror to my mind. We did not preach (which of us would have listened?), but we followed in fancy, like the child, Eugénie de Guérin, those deeply coloured traditions which lent atmosphere to our simple and monotonous lives. One of our favourite games was the temptation of St. Anthony. Mariana Grognon, a little French girl of unsurpassed agility, had "created" the part of the devil. Its special feature was the flying leap she took over the kneeling hermit's head, a performance more startling than seductive. This vivacious pantomime had been frowned upon by the mistress of recreation, who had no idea what it meant, but who considered, and with reason, that Mariana was behaving like a tomboy. Then one day an overzealous St. Anthony—Marie probably—crossed himself with such suspicious fervour when the devil made his jump that the histrionic nature of the sport became evident, and it was sternly suppressed. The primitive humour of the miracle play was not in favour at the convent.

We were married in front of St. Joseph's statue, outside the chapel door, on Sunday afternoon. Sunday was selected for the ceremony, partly because we had possession of our white veils on that day,—and what bride would wear a black veil!—and partly because the greater liberty allowed us made possible an unobserved half-hour. It was Elizabeth's custom and mine to go to the chapel every Sunday before supper, and offer an earnest supplication to the Blessed Virgin that we might not be given medals that night at Primes. I loved Primes. It was the most exciting event of the week. There was an impressive solemnity about the big, hushed room, the long rows of expectant girls, Reverend Mother, begirt by the whole community, gazing at us austerely, and the seven days' record read out in Madame Bouron's clear, incisive tones. We knew how every girl in the school, even the exalted graduates and semi-sacred medallions, had behaved. We knew how they stood in class. We saw the successful students go up to receive their medals. Occasional comments from Madame Bouron added a bitter pungency to the situation. It was delightful from beginning to end, unless—and this happened very often to Elizabeth, and sometimes even to me—we had distinguished ourselves sufficiently to win our class medals for the week. *Then*, over an endless expanse of polished floor, slippery as glass, we moved like stricken creatures; conscious that our friends were watching us in mocking security from their chairs; conscious that we were swinging our arms and turning in our toes; and painfully aware that our curtsies would never come up to the required standard of elegance and grace. Elizabeth was furthermore afflicted by a dark foreboding that something—something in the nature of a stocking or a petticoat—would "come down" when she was in mid-stream, and this apprehension deepened her impenetrable gloom. It was in the hopes of averting such misery that we said our "Hail Marys" every Sunday afternoon, manifesting thereby much faith but little intelligence, as all these matters had been settled at "Conference" on Saturday.

I have always believed, however, that it was in answer to our prayers that a law was passed in mid-term, ordaining that no girl should be eligible for a class medal unless she had *all* her conduct notes, unless her week's record was without a stain. As this was sheerly impossible, we were thenceforth safe. We heard our names read out, and sat still, in disgraceful but blessed security. Even Madame Bouron's icy censure, and Reverend Mother's vaguely reproachful glance (she was hopelessly near-sighted, and hadn't the remotest idea where we sat) were easier to bear than that distressful journey up and down the classroom, with every eye upon us.

The marriage ceremony would have been more tranquil and more imposing if we had not had such a poltroon of a priest. Annie was so nervous, so afraid she was committing a sin, and so afraid she would be caught in the commission, that she read the service shamefully, and slurred all the interesting details over which we wanted to linger. Elizabeth had to prompt her repeatedly, and Tony's comments were indefensible at such a solemn hour. When the three rings had been placed upon the brides' fingers, and the three veils bashfully raised to permit the salutations of the noble grooms, we promised to meet again in the boot and shoe closet, after the dormitory lights had been lowered, and hurried back to the schoolroom. To have played our parts openly in recreation hours would have been to destroy all the pleasures of illusion. Secrecy was indispensable, secrecy and mystery; a hurried clasp of Marie's hand, as she brushed by me to her desk; a languishing glance over our dictation books in class; a tender note slipped between the pages of my grammar. I have reason to believe I was the most cherished of the three brides. Tony was not likely to expend much energy in prolonged love-making, and Emily was wholly incapable of demonstration, even if Elizabeth would have tolerated it. But Marie was dramatic to her finger-tips; she played her part with infinite grace and zeal; and I, being by nature both ardent and imitative, entered freely into her conception of our rôles. We corresponded at length, with that freedom of phrase and singleness of idea which make love letters such profitable reading.

It was in our stolen meetings, however, in those happy reunions in the boot and shoe closet, or in another stuffy hole where our hats and coats were hung, that the expansive nature of our play was made delightfully manifest. It was then that we travelled far and wide, meeting dangers with an unflinching front, and receiving everywhere the respectful welcome due to our rank and fortunes. We went to Rome, and the Holy Father greeted us with unfeigned joy. We went to Venice, and the Doge —of whose passing we were blissfully ignorant—took us a-pleasuring in the Bucentaur. Our Stuart proclivities would not permit us to visit Victoria's court,—that is, not as friends. Tony thirsted to go there and raise a row; but the young Pretender being dead (we ascertained this fact definitely from Madame Duncan, who read us a lecture on our ignorance), there seemed nobody to put in the place of the usurping queen. We crossed the desert on camels, and followed Père Huc into Tartary and Thibet. Our husbands gave us magnificent jewels, and Lilly dropped her pearl earrings into a well, like "Albuharez' Daughter" in the "Spanish Ballads." This charming mishap might have happened to me, if only I had been Princess of Castile.

Then one day Elizabeth made a discovery which filled me with confusion. Before I came to school, I had parted with my few toys, feeling that paper dolls and grace-hoops were unworthy of my new estate, and that I should never again condescend to the devices of my lonely childhood. The single exception was a small bisque doll with painted yellow curls. I had brought it to the convent in a moment of weakness, but no one was aware of its existence. It was a neglected doll, nameless and wardrobeless, and its sole function was to sleep with me at night. Its days were spent in solitary confinement in my washstand drawer. This does not mean that evening brought any sense of exile to my heart. On the contrary, the night fears which at home made going to bed an ever repeated misery (I slept alone on a big, echoing third floor, and everybody said what a brave little girl I was) had been banished by the security of the dormitory, by the blessed sense of companionship and protection. Nevertheless, I liked to feel my doll in bed with me, and I might have enjoyed its secret and innocent society all winter, had I not foolishly carried it downstairs one day in my pocket, and stowed it in a corner of my desk. The immediate consequence was detection.

"How did you come to have it?" asked Elizabeth, wondering.

"Oh, it got put in somehow with my things," I answered evasively, and feeling very much ashamed.

Elizabeth took the poor little toy, and looked at it curiously. She must have possessed such things once, but it was as hard to picture her with a doll as with a rattle. She seemed equally remote from both. As she turned it over, an inspiration came to her. "I tell you what we'll do," she said; "we'll take it for your baby,—it's time one of us had a child,—and we'll get up a grand christening. Do you want a son or a daughter?"

"I hope we won't have Annie Churchill for a priest," was my irrelevant answer.

"No, we won't," said Elizabeth. "I'll be the priest, and Tony and Lilly can be godparents. And then, after its christening, the baby can die,—in its baptismal innocence, you know,—and we'll bury it."

I was silent. Elizabeth raised her candid eyes to mine. "You don't want it, do you?" she asked.

"I don't want it," I answered slowly.

Marie decided that, as our first-born was to die, it had better be a girl. A son and heir should live to inherit the estates. She contributed a handkerchief for a christening robe; and Emily, who was generous to a fault, insisted on giving a little new work-basket, beautifully lined with blue satin, for a coffin. Lilly found a piece of white ribbon for a sash. Tony gave advice, and Elizabeth her priestly benediction. Beata Benedicta della Rovere ("That name shows she's booked for Heaven," said Tony) was christened in the *bénitier* at the chapel door; Elizabeth performing the ceremony, and Tony and Lilly unctuously renouncing in her behalf the works and pomps of Satan. It was a more seemly service than our wedding had been, but it was only a prelude, after all, to the imposing rites of burial. These were to take place at the recreation hour the following afternoon; but owing to the noble infant's noble kinsmen not having any recreation hour when the afternoon came, the obsequies were unavoidably postponed.

It happened in this wise. Every day, in addition to our French classes, we had half an hour of French conversation, at which none of us ever willingly conversed. All efforts to make us sprightly and loquacious failed signally. When questions were put to us, we answered them; but we never embarked of our own volition upon treacherous currents of speech. Therefore Madame Davide levied upon us a conversational tax, which, like some of the most oppressive taxes the world has ever known, made a specious pretence of being a voluntary contribution. Every girl in the class was called upon to recount some anecdote, some incident or story which she had heard, or read, or imagined, and which she was supposed to be politely eager to communicate to her comrades. We always began "Madame et mesdemoiselles, figurez-vous," or "il y avait une fois," and then launched ourselves feebly upon tales, the hopeless inanity of which harmonized with the spiritless fashion of the telling. We all felt this to be a degrading performance. Our tender pride was hurt by such a betrayal, before our friends, of our potential imbecility. Moreover, the strain upon invention and memory was growing daily more severe. We really had nothing left to tell. Therefore five of us (Marie belonged to a higher class) resolved to indicate that our resources were at an end by telling the same story over and over again. We selected for this purpose an Ollendorfian anecdote about a soldier in the army of Frederick the Great, who, having a watch chain but no watch, attached a bullet—I can't conceive how—to the chain; and, when Frederick asked him the hour of the day, replied fatuously: "My watch tells me that any hour is the time to die for your majesty."

The combined improbability and stupidity of this tale commended it for translation, and the uncertainty as to the order of the telling lent an element of piquancy to the plot. Happily for Lilly, she was called upon first to "réciter un conte," and, blushing and hesitating, she obeyed. Madame Davide listened with a pretence of interest that did her credit, and said that the soldier had "beaucoup d'esprit;" at which Tony, who had pronounced him a fool, whistled a soft note of incredulity. After several other girls had enlivened the class with mournful pleasantries, my turn came, and I told the story as fast as I could,—so fast that its character was not distinctly recognized until the last word was said. Madame Davide looked puzzled, but let it pass. Perhaps she thought the resemblance accidental. But when Emily with imperturbable gravity began: "Il y avait une fois un soldat, honnête et brave, dans l'armée de Frédéric le Grand," and proceeded with the familiar details, she was sharply checked. "Faut pas répéter les mêmes contes," said Madame Davide; at which Emily, virtuous and pained, explained that it was *her* conte. How could she help it if other girls chose it too? By this time the whole class had awakened to the situation, and was manifesting the liveliest interest and pleasure. It was almost pitiful to see children so grateful for a little mild diversion. Like the gratitude of Italian beggars for a few sous, it indicated painfully the desperate nature of their needs. There was a breathless gasp of expectancy when Elizabeth's name was called. We knew we could trust Elizabeth. She was constitutionally incapable of a blunder. Every trace of expression was banished from her face, and in clear, earnest tones she said: "Madame et mesdemoiselles,— il y avait une fois un soldat, honnête et brave, dans l'armée de Frédéric le Grand,"—whereupon there arose a shout of such uncontrollable delight that the class was dismissed, and we were all sent to our desks. Tony alone was deeply chagrined. Through no fault of hers, she was for once out of a scrape, and she bitterly resented the exclusion. It was in consequence of this episode that Beata Benedicta's funeral rites were postponed for twenty-four hours.

The delay brought no consolation to my heart. It only prolonged my unhappiness. I did not love my doll after the honest fashion of a younger child. I did not really fear that I should miss her. But, what was infinitely worse, I could not bring myself to believe that Beata Benedicta was dead, —although I was going to allow her to be buried. The line of demarcation between things that can feel and things that cannot had always been a wavering line for me. Perhaps Hans Andersen's stories, in which rush-lights and darning needles have as much life as boys and girls, were responsible for my mental confusion. Perhaps I merely held on longer than most children to a universal instinct which they share with savages. Any familiar object, anything that I habitually handled, possessed some portion of my own vitality. It was never wholly inanimate. Beata's little bisque body, with its outstretched arms, seemed to protest mutely but piteously against abandonment. She had lain by my side for months, and now I was going to let her be buried alive, because I was ashamed to rescue her. There was no help for it. Rather than confess I was such a baby, I would have been buried myself.

A light fall of snow covered the frozen earth when we dug Beata's grave with our penknives, and laid her mournfully away. The site selected was back of the "Seven Dolours" chapel (chapels are to convent grounds what arbours and summer-houses are to the profane), and we chose it because the friendly walls hid us from observation. We had brought out our black veils, and we put them on over our hats, in token of our heavy grief. Elizabeth read the burial service,—or as much of it as she deemed prudent, for we dared not linger too long,—and afterwards reassured us on the subject of Beata's baptismal innocence. That was the great point. She had died in her sinless infancy. We crime-laden souls should envy her happier fate. We put a little cross of twigs at the head of the grave, and promised to plant something there when the spring came. Then we took off our veils, and stuffed them in our pockets,—those deep, capacious pockets of many years ago.

"Let's race to the avenue gate," said Tony. "I'm frozen stiff. Burying is cold work."

"Or we might get one of the swings," said Lilly.

But Marie—whose real name, I forgot to say, was Francesco—put her arm tenderly around me. "Don't grieve, Beatrice," she said. "Our little Beata has died in her baptismal"—

"Oh, come away!" I cried, unable to bear the repetition of this phrase. And I ran as fast as I could down the avenue. But I could not run fast enough to escape from the voice of Beata Benedicta, calling—calling to me from her grave.

Reverend Mother's Feast

"Mother's feast"—in other words the saint's day of the Superioress—was dawning upon our horizon, and its lights and shadows flecked our checkered paths. Theoretically, it was an occasion of pure joy, assuring us, as it did, a *congé*, and not a *congé* only, but the additional delights of a candy fair in the morning, and an operetta, "The Miracle of the Roses," at night. Such a round of pleasures filled us with the happiest anticipations; but—on the same principle that the Church always prefaces her feast days with vigils and with fasts—the convent prefaced our *congé* with a competition in geography, and with the collection of a "spiritual bouquet," which was to be our offering to Reverend Mother on her fête.

A competition in anything was an unqualified calamity. It meant hours of additional study, a frantic memorizing of facts, fit only to be forgotten, and the bewildering ordeal of being interrogated before the whole school. It meant for *me* two little legs that shook like reeds, a heart that thumped like a hammer in my side, a sensation of sickening terror when the examiner—Madame Bouron—bore down upon me, and a mind reduced to sudden blankness, washed clean of any knowledge upon any subject, when the simplest question was asked. Tried by this process, I was only one degree removed from idiocy. Even Elizabeth, whose legs were as adamant, whose heart-beats had the regularity of a pendulum, and who, if she knew a thing, could say it, hated to bound states and locate capitals for all the school to hear. "There are to be prizes, too," she said mournfully. "Madame Duncan said so. I don't like going up for a prize. It's worse than a medal at Primes."

"Oh, well, maybe you won't get one," observed Tony consolingly. "You didn't, you know, last time."

"I did the time before last," said Elizabeth calmly. "It was 'La Corbeille de Fleurs.'"

There was an echo of resentment in her voice, and we all—even Tony—admitted that she had just cause for complaint. To reward successful scholarship with a French book was one of those black-hearted deeds for which we invariably held Madame Bouron responsible. She may have been blameless as the babe unborn; but it was our habit to attribute all our wrongs to her malign influence. We knew "La Corbeille de Fleurs." At least, we knew its shiny black cover, and its frontispiece, representing a sylphlike young lady in a floating veil bearing a hamper of provisions to a smiling and destitute old gentleman. There was nothing in this picture, nor in the accompanying lines, "Que vois-je? Mon Dieu! Un ange de Ciel, qui vient à mon secours," which tempted us to a perusal of the story, even had we been in the habit of voluntarily reading French.

As for the "spiritual bouquet," we felt that our failure to contribute to it on a generous scale was blackening our reputations forever. Every evening the roll was called, and girl after girl gave in her list of benefactions. Rosaries, so many. Litanies, so many. Aspirations, so many. Deeds of kindness, so many. Temptations resisted, so many. Trials offered up, so many. Acts, so many. A stranger, listening to the replies, might have imagined that the whole school was ripe for Heaven. These blossoms of virtue and piety were added every night to the bouquet; and the sum total, neatly written out in Madame Duncan's flowing hand, was to be presented, with an appropriate address, to Reverend Mother on her feast, as a proof of our respectful devotion.

It was a heavy tax. From what resources some girls drew their supplies remained ever a mystery to us. How could Ellie Plunkett have found the opportunity to perform four deeds of kindness, and resist seven temptations, in a day? We never had any temptations to resist. Perhaps when one came along, we yielded to it so quickly that it had ceased to tempt before its true character had been ascertained. And to whom was Ellie Plunkett so overweeningly kind? "Who wants Ellie Plunkett to be kind to her?" was Tony's scornful query. There was Adelaide Harrison, too, actually turning in twenty acts as one day's crop, and smiling modestly when Madame Duncan praised her self-denial. Yet, to our unwarped judgment, she seemed much the same as ever. We, at least, refused to accept her estimate of her own well-spent life.

"Making an act" was the convent phraseology for doing without something one wanted, for stopping short on the verge of an innocent gratification. If I gave up my place in the swing to Viola Milton, that was an act. If I walked to the woods with Annie Churchill, when I wanted to walk with Elizabeth, that was an act. If I ate my bread unbuttered, or drank my tea unsweetened, that was an act. It will be easily understood that the constant practice of acts deprived life of everything that made it worth the living. We were so trained in this system of renunciation that it was impossible to enjoy even the very simple pleasures that our convent table afforded. If there were anything we particularly liked, our nagging little consciences piped up with their intolerable "Make an act, make an act;" and it was only when the last mouthful was resolutely swallowed that we could feel sure we had triumphed over asceticism. There was something maddening in the example set us by our neighbours, by those virtuous and pious girls who hemmed us in at study time and at our meals. When Mary Rawdon gently waved aside the chocolate custard—which was the very best chocolate custard it has ever been my good fortune to eat—and whispered to me as she did so, "An act for the bouquet;" I whispered back, "Take it, and give it to me," and held out my plate with defiant greed. Annie Churchill told us she hadn't eaten any butter for a week; whereat Tony called her an idiot, and Annie—usually the mildest of girls—said that "envy at another's spiritual good" was a very great sin, and that Tony had committed it. There is nothing so souring to the temper as abstinence.

What made it singularly hard to sacrifice our young lives for the swelling of a spiritual bouquet was that Reverend Mother, who was to profit by our piety, had so little significance in our eyes. She was as remote from the daily routine of the school as the Grand Lama is remote from the humble Thibetans whom he rules; and if we regarded her with a lively awe, it was only because of her aloofness, of the reserves that hedged her majestically round. She was an Englishwoman of good family, and of vast bulk. There was a tradition that she had been married and widowed before she became a nun; but this was a subject upon which we were not encouraged to talk. It was considered both disrespectful and indecorous. Reverend Mother's voice was slow and deep, a ponderous voice to suit her ponderous size; and she spoke with what seemed to us a strange and barbarous accent, pronouncing certain words in a manner which I have since learned was common in the days of Queen Elizabeth, and which a few ripe scholars are now endeavouring to reintroduce. She was nearsighted to the verge of blindness, and always at Mass used a large magnifying glass, like the one held by Leo the Tenth in Raphael's portrait. She was not without literary tastes of an insipid and obsolete order, the tastes of an English gentlewoman, reared in the days when young ladies read the "Female Spectator," and warbled "Oh, no, we never mention her." Had she not "entered religion," she might have taken Moore and Byron to her heart,—as did one little girl whose "Childe Harold" lay deeply hidden in a schoolroom desk,—but the rejection of these profane poets had left her stranded upon such feeble substitutes as Letitia Elizabeth Landon, whose mysterious death she was occasionally heard to deplore.

Twice on Sundays Reverend Mother crossed our orbit; in the morning, when she instructed the whole school in Christian doctrine, and at night, when she presided over Primes. During the week we saw her only at Mass. We should never even have known about Letitia Elizabeth Landon, had she not granted an occasional audience to the graduates, and discoursed to them sleepily upon the books she had read in her youth. Whatever may have been her qualifications for her post (she had surpassing dignity of carriage, and was probably a woman of intelligence and force), to us she was a mere embodiment of authority, as destitute of personal malice as of personal charm. I detested Madame Bouron, and loved Madame Rayburn. Elizabeth detested Madame Bouron, and loved Madame Dane. Emily detested Madame Bouron, and loved Madame

Duncan. These were emotions, amply nourished, and easily understood. We were capable of going to great lengths to prove either our aversion or our love. But to give up chocolate custard for Reverend Mother was like suffering martyrdom for a creed we did not hold.

"It's because Reverend Mother is so fond of geography that we're going to have the competition," said Lilly. "Madame Duncan told me so."

"Why can't Reverend Mother, if she likes it so much, learn it for herself?" asked Tony sharply. "I'll lend her my atlas."

"Oh, she knows it all," said Lilly, rather scandalized. "Madame Duncan told me it was her favourite study, and that she knew the geography of the whole world."

"Then I don't see why she wants to hear us say it," observed Elizabeth, apparently under the impression that competitions, like gladiatorial shows, were gotten up solely for the amusement of an audience. It never occurred to her, nor indeed to any of us, to attach any educational value to the performance. We conceived that we were butchered to make a convent holiday.

"And it's because Reverend Mother is so fond of music that we are going to have an operetta instead of a play," went on Lilly, pleased to have information to impart.

I sighed heavily. How could anybody prefer anything to a play? I recognized an operetta as a form of diversion, and was grateful for it, as I should have been grateful for any entertainment, short of an organ recital. We were none of us surfeited with pleasures. But to me song was at best only an imperfect mode of speech; and the meaningless repetition of a phrase, which needed to be said but once, vexed my impatient spirit. We were already tolerably familiar with "The Miracle of the Roses." For two weeks past the strains had floated from every music room. We could hear, through the closed doors, Frances Fenton, who was to be St. Elizabeth of Hungary, quavering sweetly,—

"Unpretending and lowly,

Like spirits pure and holy,

I love the wild rose best,

I love the wild rose best,

I love the wi-i-ild rose best."

We could hear Ella Holrook announcing in her deep contralto,—

"'Tis the privilege of a Landgrave

To go where glory waits him,

Glory waits him;"

and the chorus trilling jubilantly,—

"Heaven has changed the bread to roses,

Heaven has changed the bread to roses."

Why, I wondered, did they have to say everything two and three times over? Even when the Landgrave detects St. Elizabeth in the act of carrying the loaves to the poor, his anger finds a vent in iteration.

"Once again you've dared to brave my anger,

Yes, once again you've dared to brave my anger;

My power you scorn,

My power you scorn."

To which the Saint replies gently, but tediously,—

"My lord they are,

My lord they are

But simple roses,

But simple ro-o-oses,

That I gathered in the garden even now."

"Suppose that bread hadn't been changed to roses," said Elizabeth speculatively, "I wonder what St. Elizabeth would have done."

"Oh, she knew it had been, because she prayed it would be," said Marie, who was something of a theologian.

"But suppose it hadn't."

"But it *had*, and she knew it had, because of her piety and faith," insisted Marie.

"I shouldn't have liked to risk it," murmured Elizabeth.

"*I* think her husband was a pig," said Tony. "Going off to the Crusade, and making all that fuss about a few loaves of bread. If I'd been St. Elizabeth"—

She paused, determining her course of action, and Marie ruthlessly interposed. "If you're not a saint, you can't tell what you would do if you were a saint. You would be different."

There was no doubt that Tony as a saint would have to be so very different from the Tony whom we knew, that Marie's dogmatism prevailed. Even Elizabeth was silenced; and, in the pause that followed, Lilly had a chance to impart her third piece of information. "It's because Reverend Mother's name is Elizabeth," she said, "that we're going to have an operetta about St. Elizabeth; and Bessie Treves is to make the address."

"Thank Heaven, there is another Elizabeth in the school, or I might have to do it," cried our Elizabeth, who coveted no barren honours; and—even as she spoke—the blow fell. Madame Rayburn appeared at the schoolroom door, a folded paper in her hand. "Elizabeth," she said, and, with a hurried glance of apprehension, the saint's unhappy namesake withdrew. We looked at one another meaningly. "It's like giving thanks before you're sure of dinner," chuckled Tony.

I had no chance to hear any particulars until night, when Elizabeth watched her opportunity, and sallied forth to brush her teeth while I was dawdling over mine. The strictest silence prevailed in the dormitories, and no child left her alcove except for the ceremony of tooth-brushing, which was performed at one of two large tubs, stationed in the middle of the floor. These tubs—blessed be their memory!—served as centres of gossip. Friend met friend, and smothered confidences were exchanged. Our gayest witticisms,—hastily choked by a toothbrush,—our oldest and dearest jests were whispered brokenly to the accompaniment of little splashes of water. It was the last social event of our long social day, and we welcomed it as freshly as if we had not been in close companionship since seven o'clock in the morning. Elizabeth, scrubbing her teeth with ostentatious vigour, found a chance to tell me, between scrubs, that Bessie Treves had been summoned home for a week, and that she, as the only other bearer of Reverend Mother's honoured name, had been chosen to make the address. "It's the feast of St. Elizabeth," she whispered, "and the operetta is about St. Elizabeth, and they want an Elizabeth to speak. I wish I had been christened Melpomene."

"You couldn't have been christened Melpomene," I whispered back, keeping a watchful eye upon Madame Chapelle, who was walking up and down the dormitory, saying her beads. "It isn't a Christian name. There never was a St. Melpomene."

"It's nearly three pages long," said Elizabeth, alluding to the address, and not to the tragic Muse. "All about the duties of women, and how they ought to stay at home and be kind to the poor, like St. Elizabeth, and let their husbands go to the Crusades."

"But there are no Crusades any more for their husbands to go to," I objected.

Elizabeth looked at me restively. She did not like this fractious humour. "I mean let their husbands go to war," she said.

"But if there are no wars," I began, when Madame Chapelle, who had not been so inattentive as I supposed, intervened. "Elizabeth and Agnes, go back to your alcoves," she said. "You have been quite long enough brushing your teeth."

I flirted my last drops of water over Elizabeth, and she returned the favour with interest, having more left in her tumbler than I had. It was our customary good-night. Sometimes, when we were wittily disposed, we said "*Asperges me*." That was one of the traditional jests of the convent. Generations of girls had probably said it before us. Our language was enriched with scraps of Latin and apt quotations, borrowed from Church services, the Penitential Psalms, and the catechism.

For two days Elizabeth studied the address, and for two days more she rehearsed it continuously under Madame Rayburn's tutelage. At intervals she recited portions of it to us, and we favoured her with our candid criticisms. Tony objected vehemently to the very first line:—

"A woman's path is ours to humbly tread."

She said she didn't intend to tread it humbly at all; that Elizabeth might be as humble as she pleased (Elizabeth promptly disclaimed any personal sympathy with the sentiment), and that Marie and Agnes were welcome to all the humility they could practise (Marie and Agnes rejected their share of the virtue), but that she—Tony—was tired of behaving like an affable worm. To this, Emily, with more courage than courtesy, replied that a worm Tony might be, but an affable worm, never; and Elizabeth headed off any further retort by hurrying on with the address.

"A woman's path is ours to humbly tread,

And yet to lofty heights our hopes are led.

We may not share the Senate's stern debate,

Nor guide with faltering hand the helm of state;

Ours is the holier right to soften party hate,

And teach the lesson, lofty and divine,

Ambition's fairest flowers are laid at Virtue's shrine."

"Have you any idea what all that means?" asked Marie discontentedly.

"Oh, I don't have to say what it means," returned Elizabeth, far too sensible to try to understand anything she would not be called upon to explain. "Reverend Mother makes that out for herself."

"Not ours the right to guide the battle's storm,

Where strength and valour deathless deeds perform.

Not ours to bind the blood-stained laurel wreath

In mocking triumph round the brow of death.

No! 'tis our lot to save the failing breath,

'Tis ours to heal each wound, and hush each moan,

To take from other hearts the pain into our own."

"It seems to me," said Tony, "that we are expected to do all the work, and have none of the fun."

"It seems to *me*," said Marie, "that by the time we have filled ourselves up with other people's pains, we won't care much about fun. Did Reverend Mother, I wonder, heal wounds and hush up moans?"

"St. Elizabeth did," explained Elizabeth. "Her husband went to the Holy Land, and was killed, and then she became a nun. There are some lines at the end, that I don't know yet, about Reverend Mother,—

'Seeking the shelter of the cloister gate,

Like the dear Saint whose name we venerate.'

Madame Rayburn wants me to make an act, and learn the rest of it at recreation this afternoon. That horrid old geography takes up all my study time."

"I've made three acts to-day," observed Lilly complacently, "and said a whole pair of beads this morning at Mass for the spiritual bouquet."

"I haven't made one act," I cried aghast. "I haven't done anything at all, and I don't know what to do."

"You might make one now," said Elizabeth thoughtfully, "and go talk to Adelaide Harrison."

I glanced at Adelaide, who was sitting on the edge of her desk, absorbed in a book. "Oh, I don't want to," I wailed.

"If you wanted to, it wouldn't be an act," said Elizabeth.

"But she doesn't want me to," I urged. "She is reading 'Fabiola.'"

"Then you'll give her the chance to make an act, too," said the relentless Elizabeth.

Argued into a corner, I turned at bay. "I won't," I said resolutely; to which Elizabeth replied: "Well, I wouldn't either, in your place," and the painful subject was dropped.

Four days before the feast the excitement had reached fever point, though the routine of school life went on with the same smooth precision. Every penny had been hoarded up for the candy fair. It was with the utmost reluctance that we bought even the stamps for our home letters, those weekly letters we were compelled to write, and which were such pale reflections of our eager and vehement selves. Perhaps this was because we knew that every line was read by Madame Bouron before it left the convent; perhaps the discipline of those days discouraged familiarity with our parents; perhaps the barrier which nature builds between the adult and the normal child was alone responsible for our lack of spontaneity. Certain it is that the stiffly written pages despatched to father or to mother every Sunday night gave no hint of our abundant and restless vitality, our zest for the little feast of life, our exaltations, our resentments, our thrice-blessed absurdities. Entrenched in the citadel of childhood, with laws of our own making, and passwords of our own devising, our souls bade defiance to the world.

If all our hopes centred in the *congé*, the candy fair, and the operetta,— which was to be produced on a scale of unwonted magnificence,—our time was sternly devoted to the unpitying exactions of geography. Every night we took our atlases to bed with us, under the impression that sleeping on a book would help us to remember its contents. As the atlases were big, and our pillows very small, this device was pregnant with discomfort. On the fourth night before the feast, something wonderful happened. It was the evening study hour, and I was wrestling sleepily with the mountains of Asia,—hideous excrescences with unpronounceable and unrememberable names,—when Madame Rayburn entered the room. As we rose to our feet, we saw that she looked very grave, and our minds took a backward leap over the day. Had we done anything unusually bad, anything that could call down upon us a public indictment, and was Madame Rayburn for once filling Madame Bouron's office? We could think of nothing; but life was full of pitfalls, and there was no sense of security in our souls. We waited anxiously.

"Children," said Madame Rayburn, "I have sorrowful news for you. Reverend Mother has been summoned to France. She sails on her feast day, and leaves for New York to-morrow."

We stared open-mouthed and aghast. The ground seemed sinking from under our feet, the walls crumbling about us. Reverend Mother sailing for France! And on her feast day, too,—the feast for which so many ardent preparations had been made. The *congé*, the competition, the address, the operetta, the spiritual bouquet, the candy fair,—were they, too, sailing away into the land of lost things? To have asked one of the questions that trembled on our lips would have been an unheard-of liberty. We listened in respectful silence, our eyes riveted on Madame Rayburn's face.

"You will all go to the chapel now," she said. "To-night we begin a novena to *Mater Admirabilis* for Reverend Mother's safe voyage. She dreads it very much, and she is sad at leaving you. Pray for her devoutly. Madame Dane will bring you down to the chapel."

She turned to go. Our hearts beat violently. She knew, she could not fail to know, the thought that was uppermost in every mind. She was too experienced and too sympathetic to miss the significance of our strained and wistful gaze. A shadowy smile crossed her face. "Madame Bouron would have told you to-morrow," she said, "what I think I shall tell you to-night. It is Reverend Mother's express desire that you should have your *congé* on her feast, though she will not be here to enjoy it with you."

A sigh of relief, a sigh which we could not help permitting to be audible, shivered softly around the room. The day was saved; yet, as we marched to the chapel, there was a turmoil of agitation in our hearts. We knew that from far-away France—from a mysterious and all-powerful person who dwelt there, and who was called Mother General—came the mandates which governed our community. This was not the first sudden departure we had witnessed; but Reverend Mother seemed so august, so permanent, so immobile. Her very size protested mutely against upheaval. Should we never again see that familiar figure sitting in her stall, peering through her glass into a massive prayer-book, a leviathan of prayer-books, as imposing in its way as she was, or blinking sleepily at us as we filed by? Why, if somebody were needed in France, had it not pleased Mother General to send for Madame Bouron? Many a dry eye would have seen *her* go. But then, as Lilly whispered to me, suppose it had been Madame Rayburn. There was a tightening of my heart-strings at the thought, a sudden suffocating pang, dimly foreboding the grief of another year.

The consensus of opinion, as gathered that evening in the dormitory, was not unlike the old Jacobite epitaph on Frederick, Prince of Wales. Every one of us was sincerely sorry that Madame Bouron had not been summoned,—

"Had it been his father,

We had much rather;"

but glad that Madame Dane, or Madame Rayburn, or Madame Duncan, or some other favourite nun had escaped.

"Since it's only Fred

Who was alive, and is dead,

There is no more to be said."

The loss of our Superioress was bewildering, but not, for us, a thing of deep concern. We should sleep as sweetly as usual that night.

The next morning we were all gathered into the big First Cours classroom, where Reverend Mother came to bid us good-by. It was a solemn leave-taking. The address was no longer in order; but the spiritual bouquet had been made up the night before, and was presented in our name by Madame Bouron, who read out the generous sum-total of prayers, and acts, and offered-up trials, and resisted temptations, which constituted our feast-day gift. As Reverend Mother listened, I saw a large tear roll slowly down her cheek, and my heart smote me—my heart was always smiting me when it was too late—that I had contributed so meagrely to the donation. I remembered the chocolate custard, and thought—for one mistaken moment—that I should never want to taste of that beloved dish again. Perhaps if I had offered it up, Reverend Mother would cross the sea in safety. Perhaps, because I ate it, she would have storms, and be drowned. The doubtful justice of this arrangement was no more apparent to me than its unlikelihood. We were accustomed to think that the wide universe was planned and run for our reward and punishment. A rainy Sunday following the misdeeds of Saturday was to us a logical sequence of events.

When the bouquet had been presented, Reverend Mother said a few words of farewell. She said them as if she were sad at heart, not only at crossing the ocean, not only at parting from her community, but at leaving us, as well. I suppose she loved us collectively. She couldn't have loved us individually, knowing us only as two long rows of uniformed, curtsying schoolgirls, whose features she was too nearsighted to distinguish. On the other hand, if our charms and our virtues were lost to her, so were our less engaging qualities. Perhaps, taken collectively, we were rather lovable. Our uniforms were spotless, our hair superlatively smooth,—no blowsy, tossing locks, as in these days of libertinism, and our curtsies as graceful as hours of practice could make them. We sank and rose like the crest of a wave. On the whole, Reverend Mother had the best of us. Madame Bouron might have been pardoned for taking a less sentimental view of the situation.

That afternoon, while we were at French class, Reverend Mother departed. We heard the carriage roll away, but were not permitted to rush to the windows and look at it, which would have been a welcome distraction from our verbs. An hour later, at recreation, Madame Rayburn sent for Elizabeth. She was gone fifteen minutes, and came back, tense with suppressed excitement.

"Oh, what is it?" we cried. "The *congé* is all right?"

"All right," said Elizabeth.

"And the candy fair?" asked Lilly, whose father had given her a dollar to squander upon sweets.

"Oh, it's all right, too. The candy is here now; and Ella Holrook and Mary Denniston and Isabel Summers are to have charge of the tables. Madame Dane told me that yesterday."

Our faces lightened, and then fell. "Is it the competition?" I asked apprehensively.

Elizabeth looked disconcerted. It was plain she knew nothing about the competition, and hated to avow her ignorance. We always felt so important when we had news to tell. "Of course, after studying all that geography, we'll have to say it sooner or later," she said. "But"—a triumphant pause—"a new Reverend Mother is coming to-morrow."

"*Ciel!*" murmured Marie, relapsing into agitated French; while Tony whistled softly, and Emily and I stared at each other in silence. The speed with which things were happening took our breath away.

"Coming to-morrow," repeated Elizabeth; "and I'm going to say the address as a welcome to her, on the night of the *congé*, before the operetta."

"Is her name Elizabeth, too?" I asked, bewildered.

"No, her name is Catherine. Madame Rayburn is going to leave out the lines about St. Elizabeth, and put in something about St. Catherine of Siena instead. That's why she wanted the address. And she is going to change the part about not sharing the Senate's stern debate, nor guiding with faltering hand the helm of state, because St. Catherine did guide the helm of state. At least, she went to Avignon, and argued with the Pope."

"Argued with the Pope!" echoed Marie, scandalized.

"She was a saint, Marie," said Elizabeth impatiently, and driving home an argument with which Marie herself had familiarized us. "She persuaded the Pope to go back to Rome. Madame Rayburn would like Kate Shaw to make the address; but she says there isn't time for another girl to study it."

"When is the feast of St. Catherine of Siena?" cried Tony, fired suddenly by a happy thought. "Maybe we'll have another *congé* then."

She rushed off to consult her prayer-book. Lilly followed her, and in a moment their two heads were pressed close together, as they scanned the Roman calendar hopefully. But before my eyes rose the image of Reverend Mother, our lost Reverend Mother, with the slow teardrop rolling down her cheek. Her operetta was to be sung to another. Her address was to be made to another. Her very saint was pushed aside in honour of another holy patroness. "The King is dead. Long live the King."

The Game of Love

It was an ancient and honourable convent custom for the little girls in the Second Cours to cultivate an ardent passion for certain carefully selected big girls in the First Cours, to hold a court of love, and vie with one another in extravagant demonstrations of affection. We were called "satellites," and our homage was understood to be of that noble and exalted nature which is content with self-immolation. No response of any kind was ever vouchsafed us. No favours of any kind were ever granted us. The objects of our devotion—ripe scholars sixteen and seventeen years old—regarded us either with good-humoured indifference or unqualified contempt. Any other line of action on their part would have been unprecedented and disconcerting. We did not want petting. We were not the lap-dog variety of children. We wanted to play the game of love according to set rules,—rules which we found in force when we came to school, and which we had no mind to alter.

Yet one of these unwritten laws—which set a limit to inconstancy—I had already broken; and Elizabeth, who was an authority on the code, offered a grave remonstrance. "We really don't change that quickly," she said with concern.

I made no answer. I had "changed" very quickly, and, though incapable of self-analysis, I was not without a dim foreboding that I would change again.

"You were wild about Isabel Summers," went on Elizabeth accusingly.

"No, I wasn't," I confessed.

"But you said you were."

Again I was silent. The one thing a child cannot do is explain a complicated situation, even to another child. How could I hope to make Elizabeth understand that, eager to worship at some shrine, I had chosen Isabel Summers with a deliberation that boded ill for my fidelity. She was a thin, blue-eyed girl, with a delicate purity of outline, and heavy braids of beautiful fair hair. Her loveliness, her sensitive temperament, her early and tragic death (she was drowned the following summer), enshrined her sweetly in our memories. She became one of the traditions of the school, and we told her tale—as of another Virginia—to all newcomers. But in the early days when I laid my heart at her feet, I knew only that she had hair like pale sunshine, and that, for a First Cours girl, she was strangely tolerant of my attentions. If I ventured to offer her the dozen chestnuts that had rewarded an hour's diligent search, she thanked me for them with a smile. If I darned her stockings with painstaking neatness,—a privilege solicited from Sister O'Neil, who had the care of our clothes,—she sometimes went so far as to commend my work. I felt that I was blessed beyond my comrades (Ella Holrook snubbed Tony, and Antoinette Mayo ignored Lilly's existence), yet there were moments when I detected a certain insipidity in the situation. It lacked the incentive of impediment.

Then in November, Julia Reynolds, who had been absent, I know not why, returned to school; and I realized the difference between cherishing a tender passion and being consumed by one, between fanning a flame and being burned. To make all this clear to Elizabeth, who was passion proof, lay far beyond my power. When she said,—

"Holy Saint Francis! what a change is here,"

—or words to that effect,—I had not even Romeo's feeble excuses to offer, though I was as obstinate as Romeo in clinging to my new love. Tony supported me, having a roving fancy of her own, and being constant to Ella Holrook, only because that imperious graduate regarded her as an intolerable nuisance.

Julia's views on the subject of satellites were even more pronounced. She enjoyed a painful popularity in the Second Cours, and there were always half a dozen children abjectly and irritatingly in love with her. She was held to be the cleverest girl in the school, a reputation skilfully maintained by an unbroken superciliousness of demeanour. Her handsome mouth was set in scornful lines; her words, except to chosen friends, were few and cold. She carried on an internecine warfare with Madame Bouron, fighting that redoubtable nun with her own weapons,—icy composure, a mock humility, and polite phrases that carried a hidden sting. It was for this, for her arrogance,—she was as contemptuous as a cat,—and for a certain elusiveness, suggestive even to my untrained mind of new and strange developments, that I surrendered to her for a season all of my heart,—all of it, at least, that was not the permanent possession of Madame Rayburn and Elizabeth.

Elizabeth was not playing the game. She was nobody's satellite just then, being occupied with a new cult for a new nun, whom it pleased her to have us all adore. The new nun, Madame Dane, was a formidable person, whom, left to myself, I should have timorously avoided; but for whom, following Elizabeth's example, I acquired in time a very creditable enthusiasm. She was tall and high-shouldered, and she had what Colly Cibber felicitously describes as a "poking head." We, who had yet to hear of Colly Cibber, admired this peculiar carriage,—Elizabeth said it was aristocratic,—and we imitated it as far as we dared, which was not very far, our shoulders being as rigorously supervised as our souls. Any indication of a stoop on *my* part was checked by an hour's painful promenade up and down the corridor, with a walking-stick held between my elbows and my back, and a heavy book balanced on my head. The treatment was efficacious. Rather than be so wearisomely ridiculous, I held myself straight as a dart.

Madame Dane, for all her lack of deportment, was the stiffest and sternest of martinets. She had a passion for order, for precision, for symmetry. It was, I am sure, a lasting grievance to her that we were of different heights, and that we could never acquire the sameness and immobility of chessmen. She did her best by arranging and rearranging us in the line of procession when we marched down to the chapel, unable to decide whether Elizabeth was a hair's breadth taller than Tony, whether Mary Aylmer and Eloise Didier matched exactly, whether Viola had better walk before Maggie McCullah, or behind her. She never permitted us to open our desks during study hours, or when we were writing our exercises. This was a general rule, but Madame Dane alone enforced it absolutely. If I forgot to take my grammar or my natural philosophy out of my desk when I sat down to work (and I was an addlepated child who forgot everything), I had to go to class with my grammar or my natural philosophy unstudied, and bear the consequences. To have borrowed my neighbour's book would have been as great a breach of discipline as to have hunted for my own. At night and morning prayers we were obliged to lay our folded hands in exactly the same position on the second rung of our chair backs. If we lifted them unconsciously to the top rung, Madame Dane swooped down upon us like a falcon upon errant doves,—which was dreadfully distracting to our devotions.

"I don't see how she stands our hair being of different lengths," said Tony. "It must worry her dreadfully. I caught her the other night eyeing Eloise Didier's long plats and my little pigtails in a most uneasy manner. Some day she'll insist on our all having it cut short, like Elizabeth and Agnes."

"That would be sensible," said Elizabeth stoutly, while Lilly put up her hands with a quick, instinctive gesture, as if to save her curly locks from destruction.

"*You* needn't talk," went on Tony with impolite emphasis, "after what you made her go through last Sunday. You and Agnes in your old black veils. I don't believe she was able to read her Mass prayers for looking at you."

Elizabeth grinned. She was not without a humorous enjoyment of the situation. Our black veils, which throughout the week were considered decorous and devotional, indicated on Sundays—when white veils were in order—a depth of unpardoned and unpardonable depravity. When Elizabeth and I were condemned to wear ours to Sunday Mass and Vespers,—two little black sheep in that vast snowy flock,—we were understood to be, for the time, moral lepers, to be cut off from spiritual communion with the elect. We were like those eminent sinners who, in the good old days when people had an eye to effect, did penance in sheets and with lighted tapers at cathedral doors,—thus adding immeasurably to the interest of church-going, and to the general picturesqueness of life. The ordeal was not for us the harrowing thing it seemed. Elizabeth's practical mind had but a feeble grasp of symbols. Burne-Jones and Maeterlinck would have conveyed no message to her, and a black veil amid the Sunday whiteness failed to disturb her equanimity. As for me, I was content to wear what Elizabeth wore. Where MacGregor sat was always the head of the table. The one real sufferer was the innocent Madame Dane, whose Sabbath was embittered by the sight of two sable spots staining the argent field, and by the knowledge that the culprits were her own Second Cours children, for whom she held herself responsible.

"She told me," said Elizabeth, "that if ever I let such a thing happen to me again, I shouldn't walk by her side all winter."

Lilly lifted her eyebrows, and Tony gave a grunt of deep significance. It meant that this would be an endurable misfortune. A cult was all very well, and Tony, like the rest of us, was prepared to play an honourable part. But Elizabeth's persistent fancy for walking by our idol's side at recreation had become a good deal of a nuisance. We considered that Madame Dane was, for a grown-up person, singularly vivacious and agreeable. She told us some of Poe's stories—notably "The Pit and the Pendulum"—in a manner which nearly stopped the beating of our hearts. We were well disposed even to her rigours. There was a straightforwardness about her methods which commended itself to our sense of justice no less than to our sense of humour. She dealt with us after fashions of her own; and, if she were constitutionally incapable of distinguishing between wilful murder and crossing one's legs in class, she would have scorned to carry any of our misdemeanours to Madame Bouron's tribunal. We felt that she had companionable qualities, rendered in some measure worthless by her advanced years; for, after all, adults have but a narrow field in which to exercise their gifts. There was a pleasant distinction in walking by Madame Dane's side up and down Mulberry Avenue, even in the unfamiliar society of Adelaide Harrison, and Mary Rawdon, who was a green ribbon, and Ellie Plunkett, who was head of the roll of honour; but it would have been much better fun to have held aloof, and have played that we were English gypsies, and that Madame Dane was Ulrica of the Banded Brow,—just then our favourite character in fiction.

Ulrica sounds, I am aware, as if she belonged in the Castle of Udolpho; but she was really a virtuous and nobly spoken outlaw in a story called "Wild Times," which was the most exciting book—the only madly exciting book—the convent library contained. It dealt with the religious persecutions of Elizabeth's glorious but stringent reign, and was a good, thorough-going piece of partisan fiction, like Fox's "Book of Martyrs," or Wodrow's "Sufferings of the Church of Scotland." I cannot now remember why Ulrica's brow was banded,—I believe she had some dreadful mark upon it,—but she was always alluding to its screened condition in words of thrilling intensity. "Seek not to know the secret of my shame. Never again shall the morning breeze nor the cool breath of evening fan Ulrica's brow."—"Tear from my heart all hope, all pity, all compunction; but venture not to lift the veil which hides forever from the eye of man the blighting token of Ulrica's shame." We loved to picture this mysterious lady—whose life, I hasten to say, was most exemplary—as tall, high-shouldered, and stern, like Madame Dane; and we merged the two characters together in a very agreeable and convincing way. It enraptured us to speak of the mistress of the Second Cours as "Ulrica," to tell one another that some day we should surely forget, and call her by that name (than which nothing was less likely), and to wonder what she would say and do if she found out the liberty we had taken.

A little private diversion of this kind was all the more necessary because the whole business of loving was essentially a public affair. Not that we were capable of voicing our affections,—Marie alone had the gift of expression,—but we ranged ourselves in solid ranks for and against the favourites of the hour. The system had its disadvantages. It deprived us of individual distinction. I was confirmed that winter, and, having found out that Madame Dane's Christian name was Theresa, I resolved to take it for my confirmation name, feeling that this was a significant proof of tenderness. Unfortunately, three other children came to the same conclusion,—Ellie Plunkett was one of them,—and the four Theresas made such an impression upon the Archbishop that he congratulated us in a really beautiful manner upon our devotion to the great saint whose name we had chosen, and whose example, he trusted, would be our beacon light.

As for my deeper and more absorbing passion for Julia Reynolds, I could not hope to separate it, or at least to make her separate it, from the passions of her other satellites. She regarded us all with a cold and impartial aversion, which was not without excuse, in view of our reprehensible behaviour. Three times a day the Second Cours filed through the First Cours classroom, on its way to the refectory. The hall was always empty, as the older girls preceded us to our meals; but at noon their hats and coats and shawls were laid neatly out upon their chairs, ready to be put on as soon as dinner was eaten. Julia Reynolds had a black and white plaid shawl, the sight of which goaded us to frenzy. If Madame Dane's eyes were turned for one instant from our ranks, some daring child shot madly across the room, wrenched a bit of fringe from this beloved shawl, and, returning in triumph with her spoil, wore it for days (I always lost mine) pinned as a love-knot to the bib of her alpaca apron. Viola Milton performed this feat so often that she became purveyor of fringe to less audacious girls, and gained honour and advantages thereby. Not content with such vandalism, she conceived the daring project of stealing a lock of hair. She hid herself in a music room, and, when Julia went by to her music lesson, stole silently behind her, and snipped off the end of one of her long brown braids. This, with the generosity of a highwayman, she distributed, in single hairs, to all who clamoured for them. To me she gave half a dozen, which I gummed up for safe-keeping in an envelope, and never saw again.

It was a little trying that Viola—certainly, as I have made plain, the least deserving of us all—should have been the only child who ever obtained a word of kindness from our divinity. But this was the irony of fate. Three days after the rape of the lock, she was sent to do penance for one of her many misdemeanours by sitting under the clock in the corridor, a post which, for some mysterious reason, was consecrated to the atonement of sin. In an hour she returned, radiant, beatified. Julia Reynolds had gone by on her way to the chapel; and seeing the little solitary figure—which looked pathetic, though it wasn't—had given her a fleeting smile, and had said "Poor Olie," as she passed.

This was hard to bear. It all came, as I pointed out acrimoniously to Tony, of Viola's being at least a head shorter than she had any business to be at ten years old, and of her having such absurdly thin legs, and great, melancholy eyes. Of course people felt sorry for her, whereas they might have known—they ought to have known—that she was incapable of being abashed. She would just as soon have sat astride the clock as under it.

One advantage, however, I possessed over all competitors. I took drawing lessons, and so did Julia Reynolds. Twice a week I sat at a table near her, and spent an hour and a half very pleasantly and profitably in watching all she did. I could not draw. My mother seemed to think that because I had no musical talent, and never in my life was able to tell one note—nor indeed one tune—from another, I must, by way of adjustment, have artistic qualities. Mr. James Payn was wont to say that his gift for mathematics consisted mainly of distaste for the classics. On precisely the same principle, I was put to draw because I could not play or sing. An all-round incapacity was, in those primitive days, a thing not wholly understood.

The only branch of my art I acquired to perfection was the sharpening of pencils and crayons; and, having thoroughly mastered this accomplishment, I ventured in a moment of temerity to ask Julia if I might sharpen hers. At first she decisively refused; but a week or two later, seeing the deftness of my work, and having a regard for her own hands, she relented, and allowed me this privilege. Henceforward I felt